BORWASSER

PLATES 2004–2008

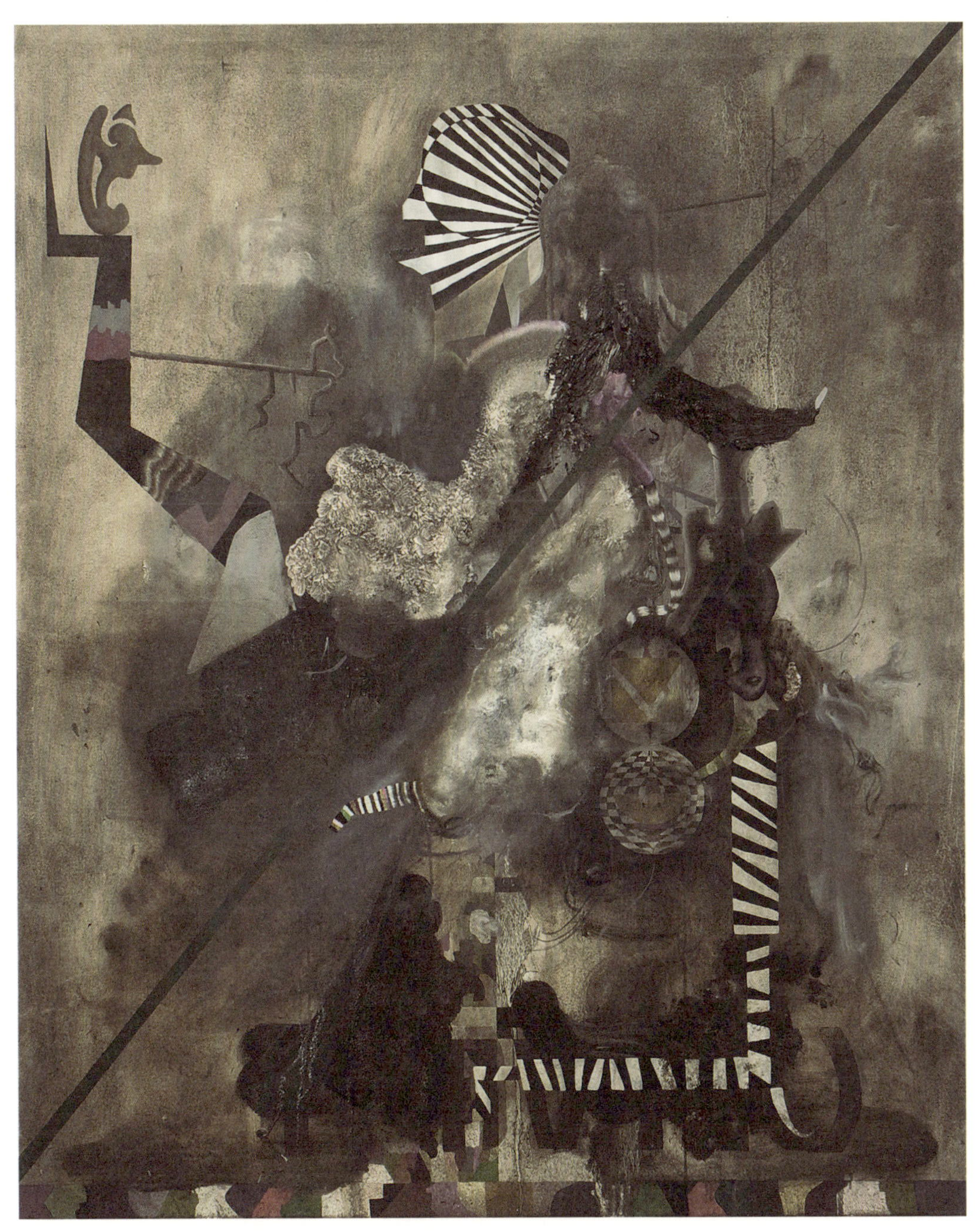

Bad Harvest, 2008, oil on canvas, 160 x 130 cm

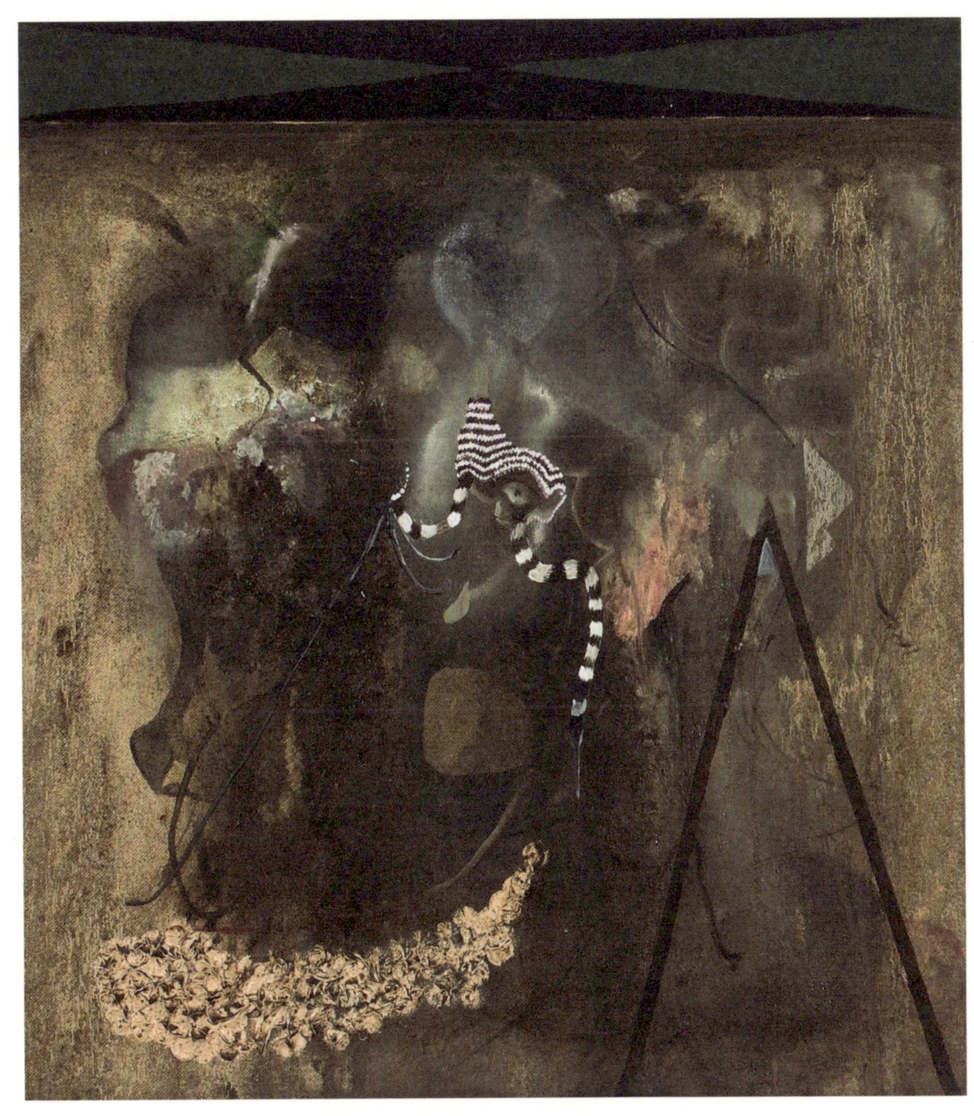

Bosskopp, 2008, oil on canvas, 50 x 45 cm

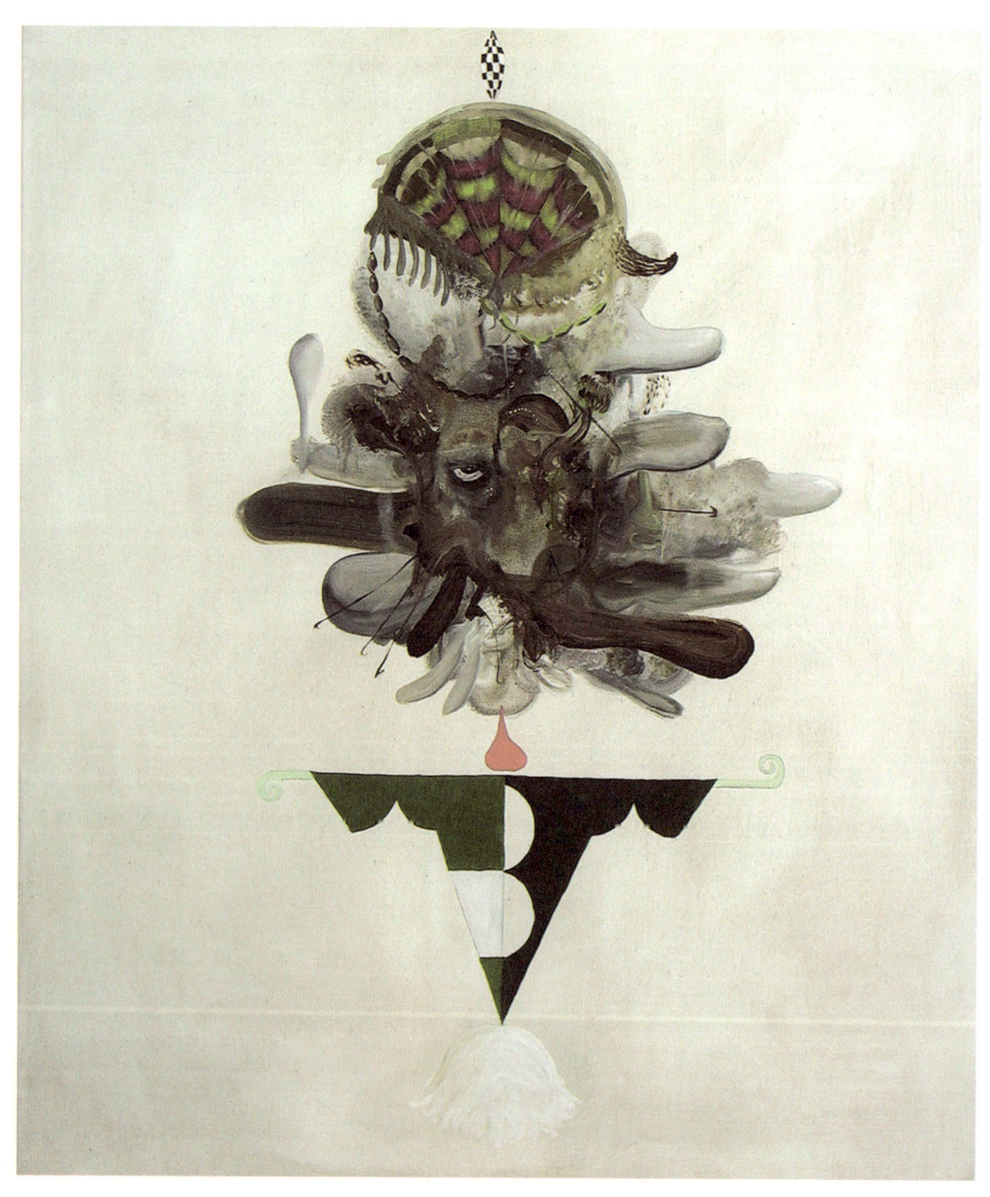

Pol 3 (Kamerad Säckle), 2005, oil on canvas, 140 x 120 cm

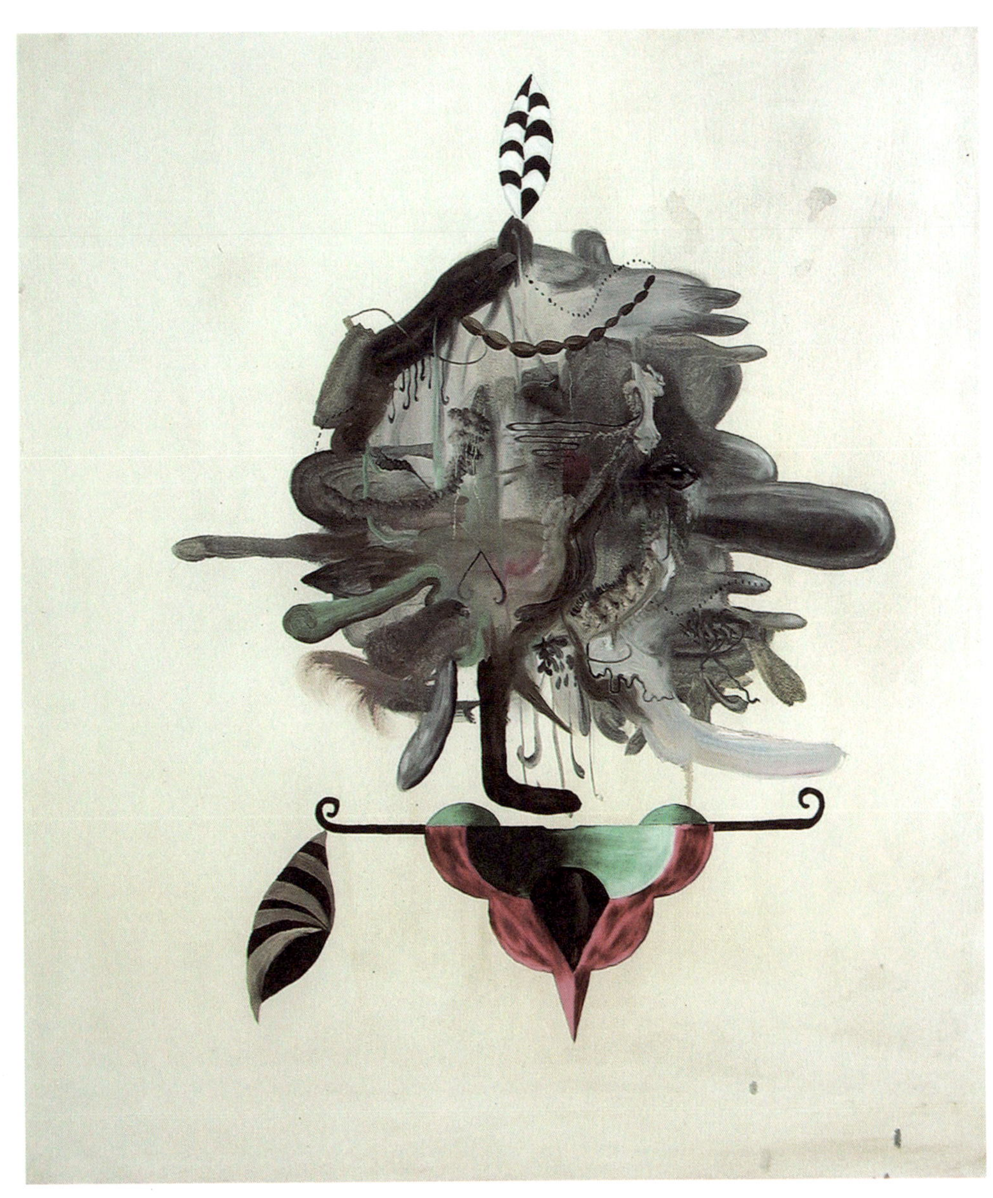

Pol 1 (Smart Estrus), 2005, oil on canvas, 140 x 120 cm

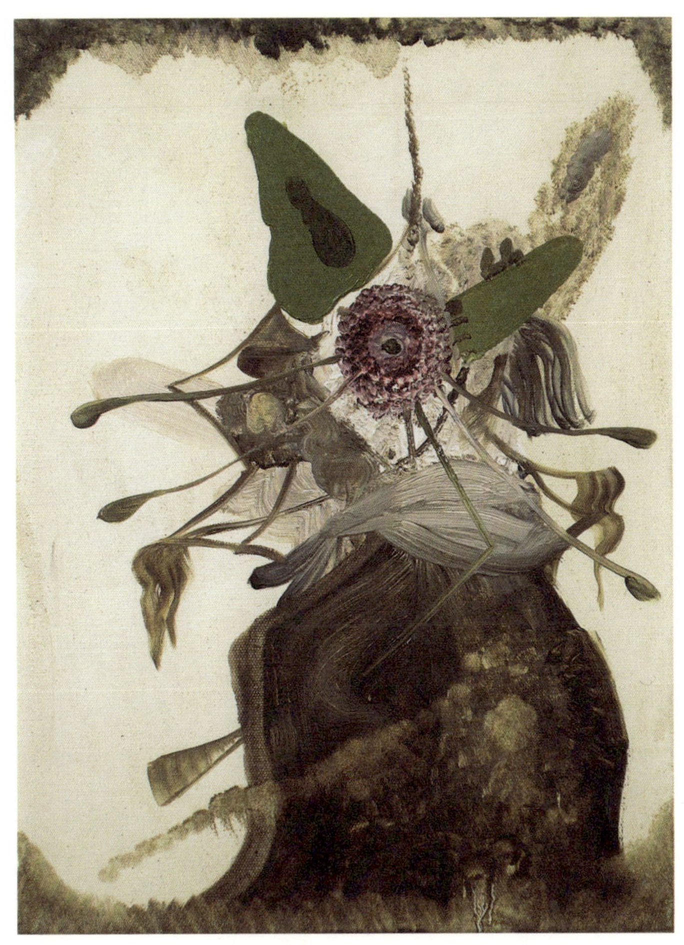

Mungo Jerry, 2006, oil on canvas, 40 x 30 cm

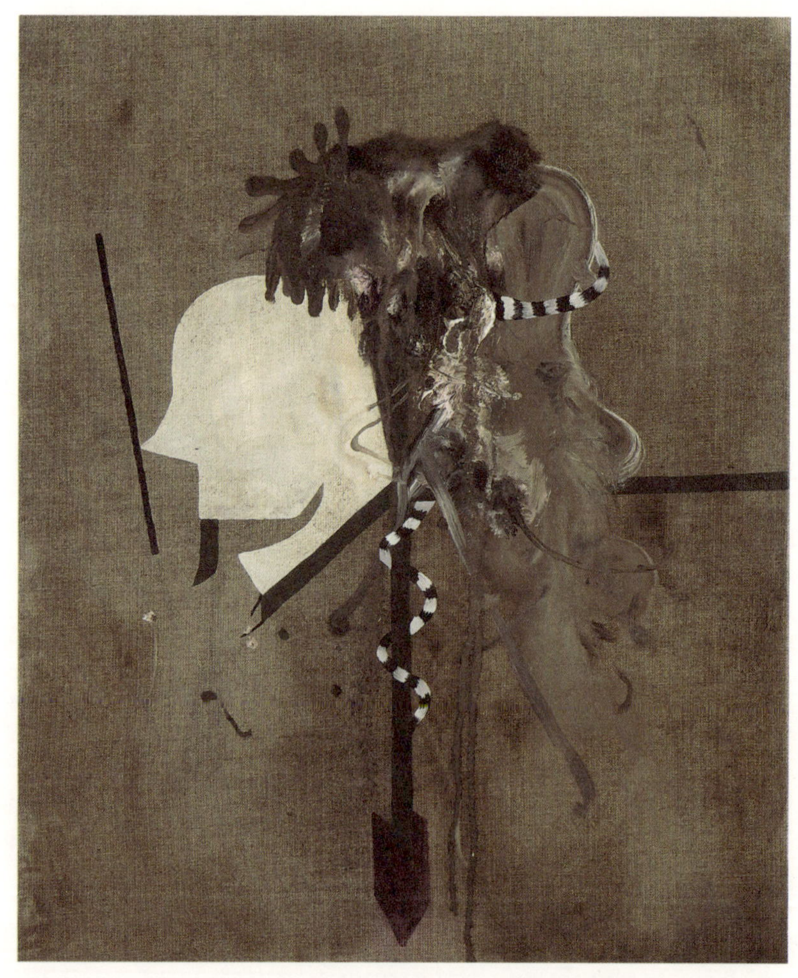

Freund 1 – deutsch, 2008, oil on canvas, 60 x 50cm

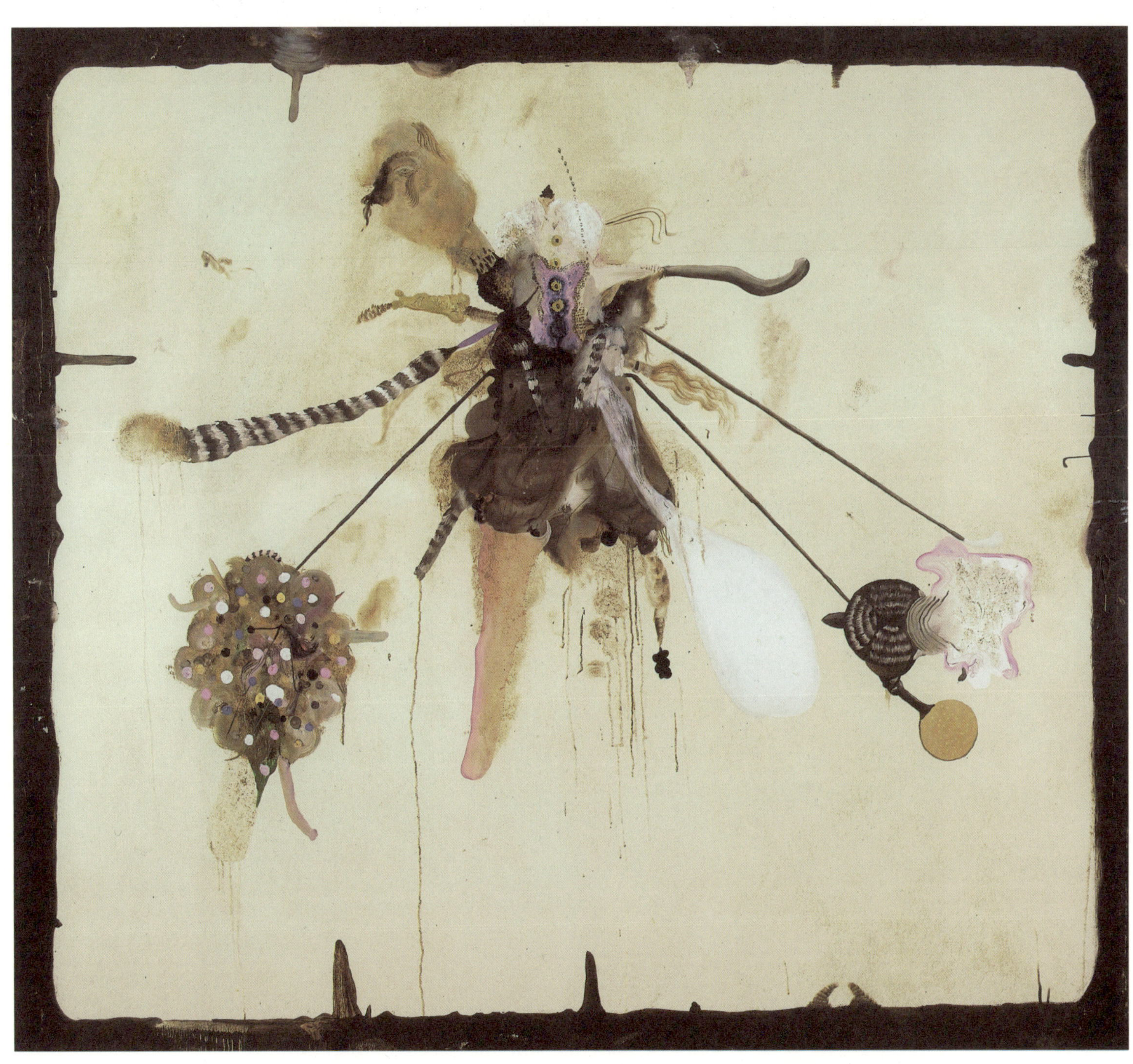

L.O.R.D.S. 8000 (der alte Haw Haw), 2006, oil on canvas, 190 x 210 cm

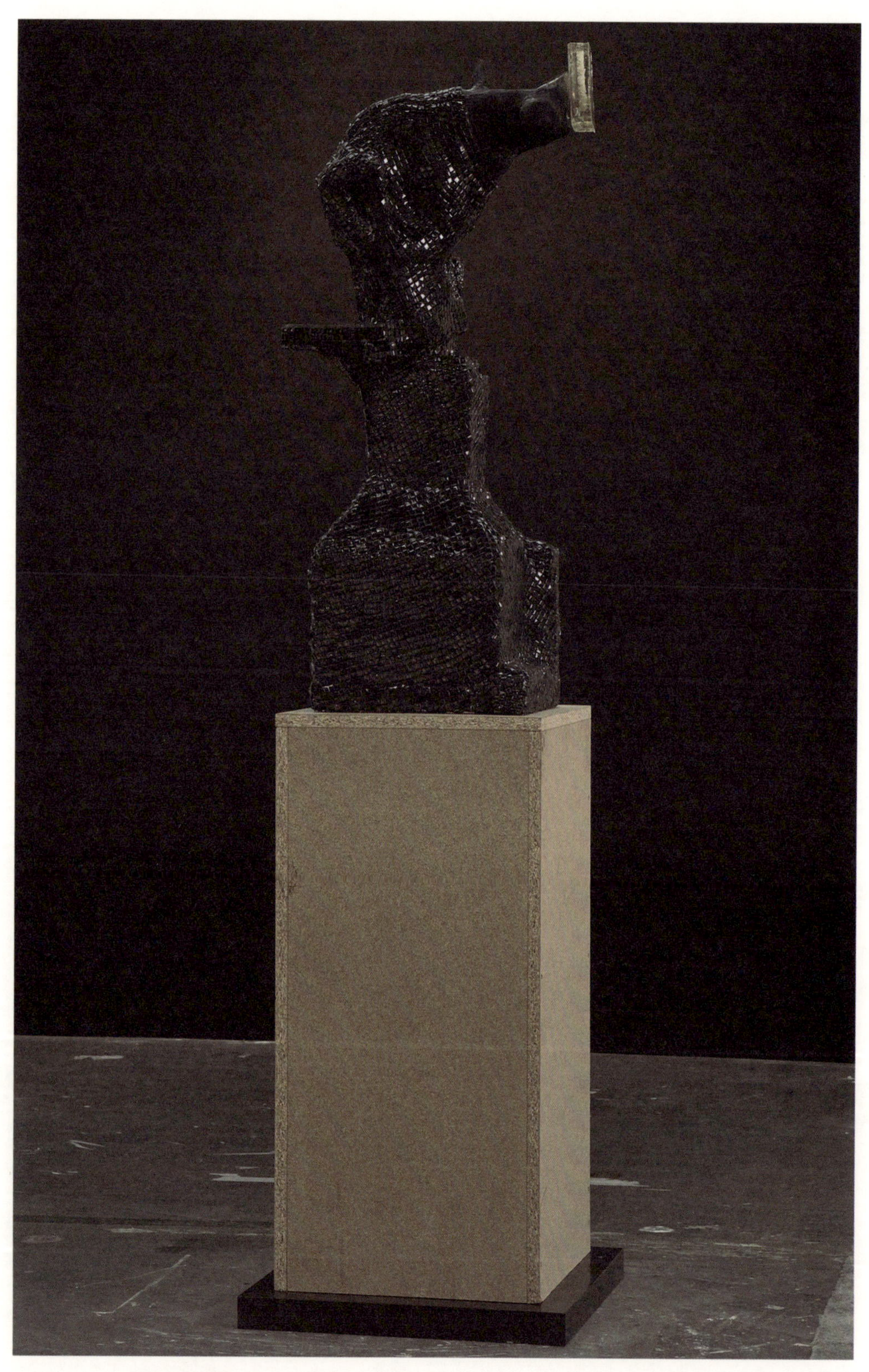

DJ El Tomorrow, 2008, glass, plaster, resin, wood, 203 x 45 x 45 cm

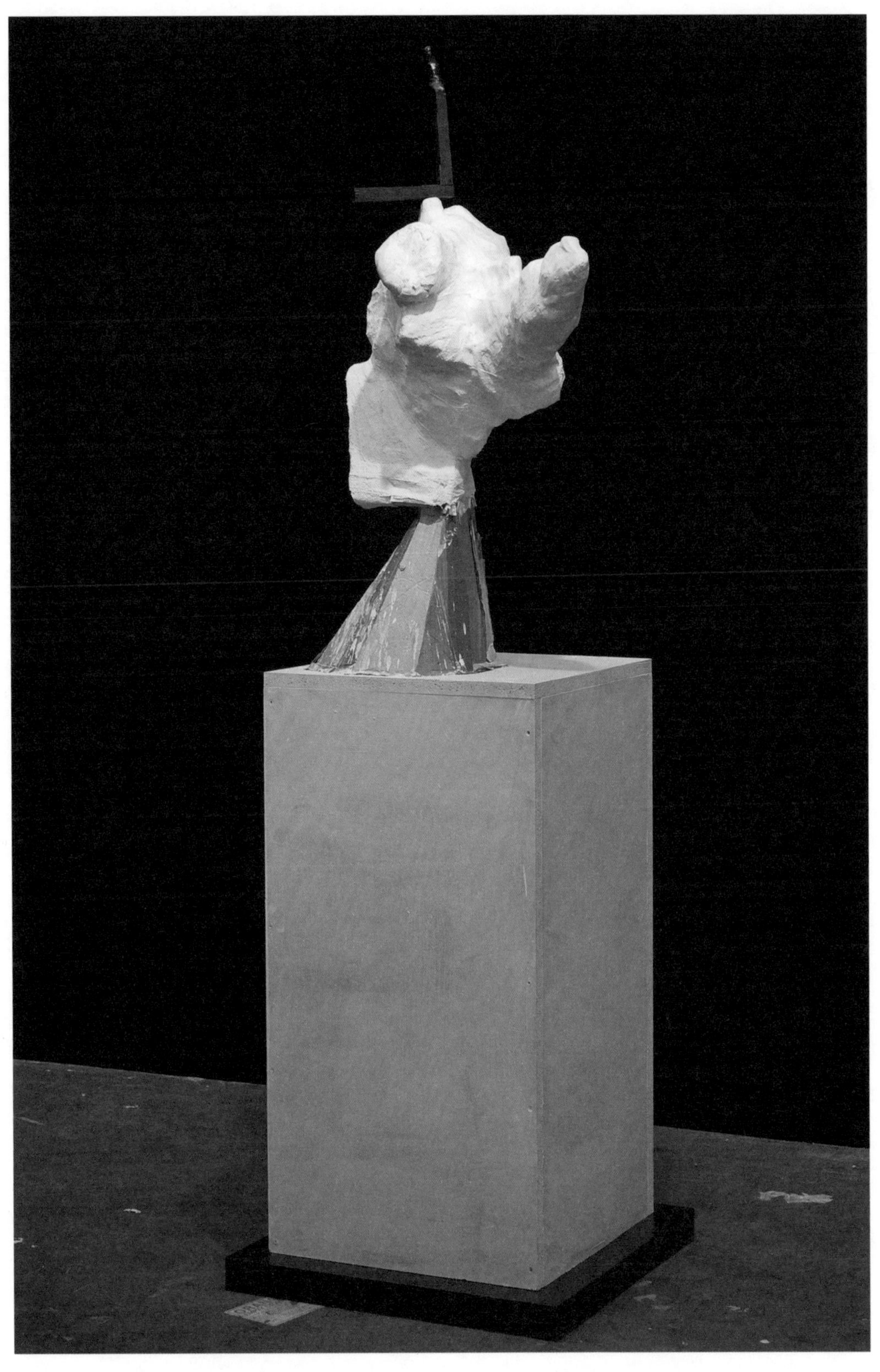

JMJ MOB, 2008, board, plaster, resin, wood, 188 x 45 x 60 cm

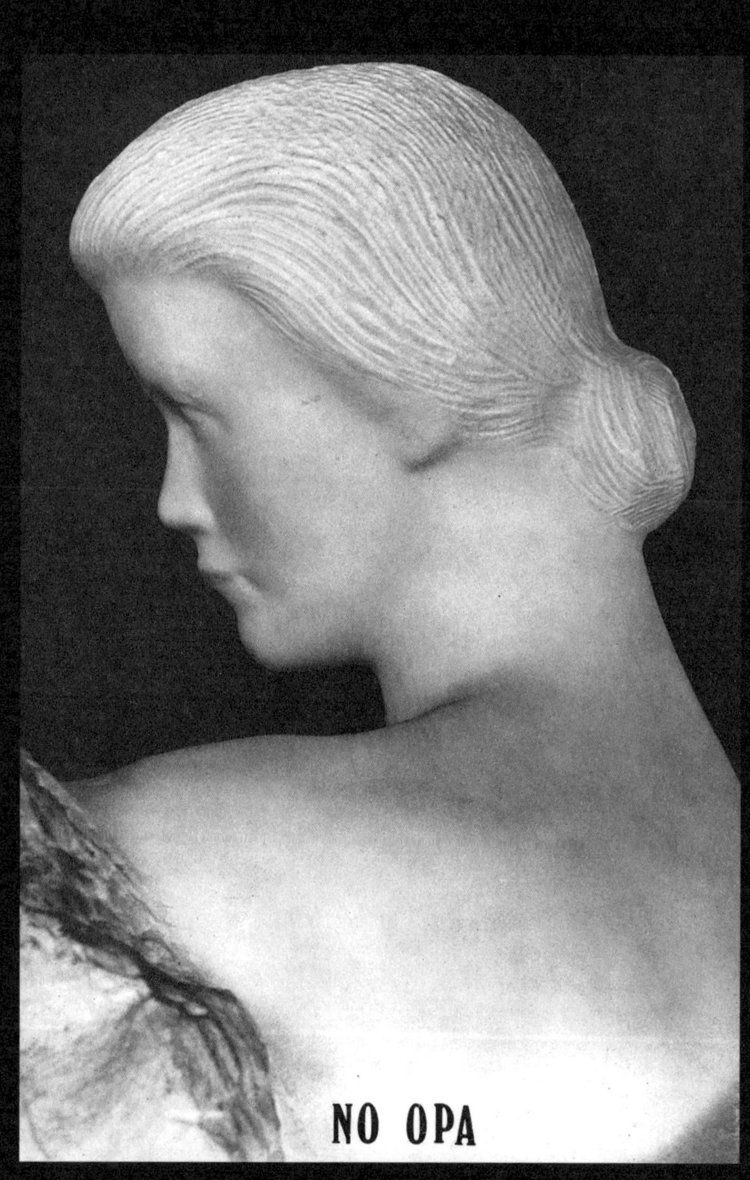
NO OPA

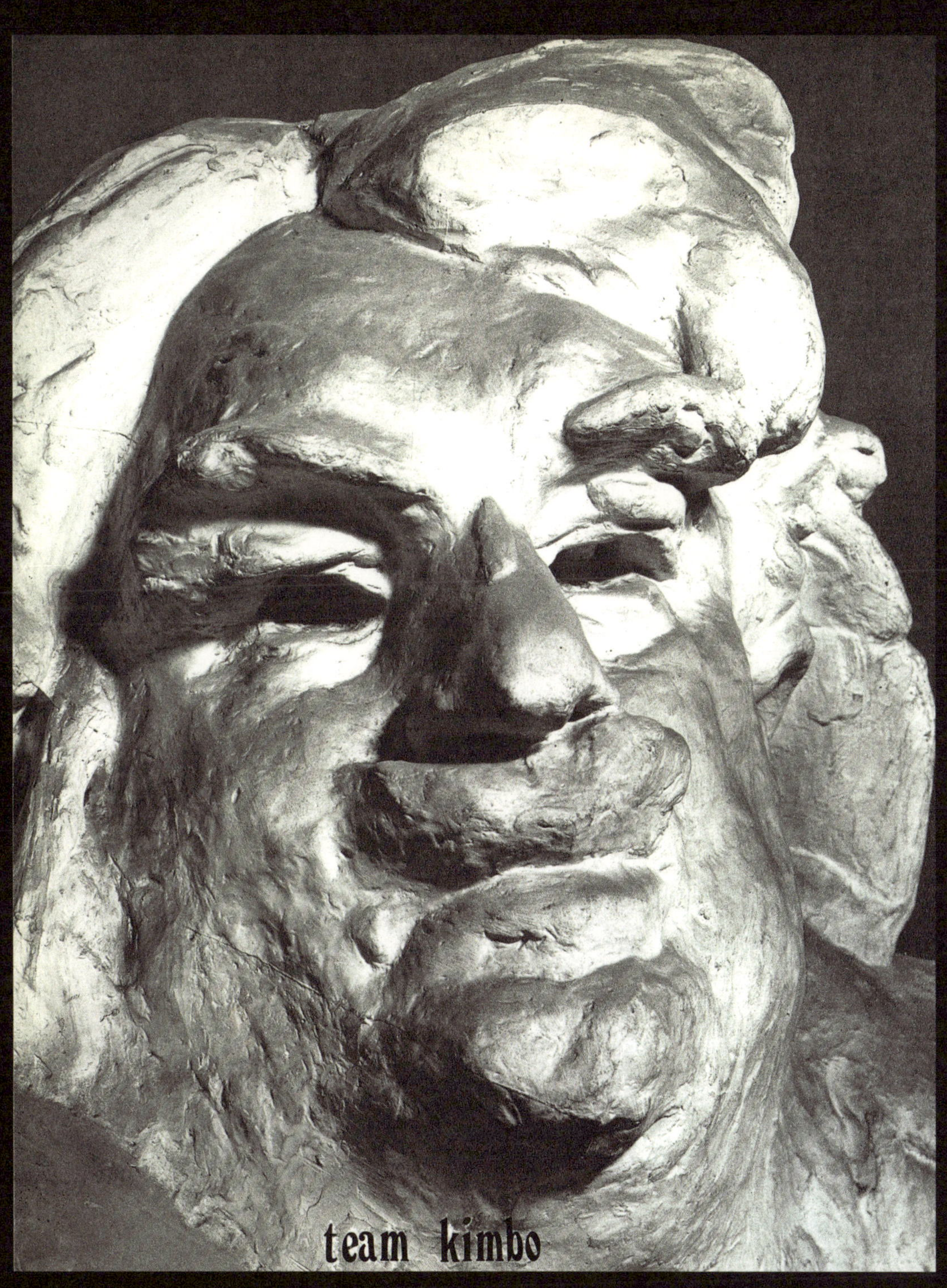
team kimbo

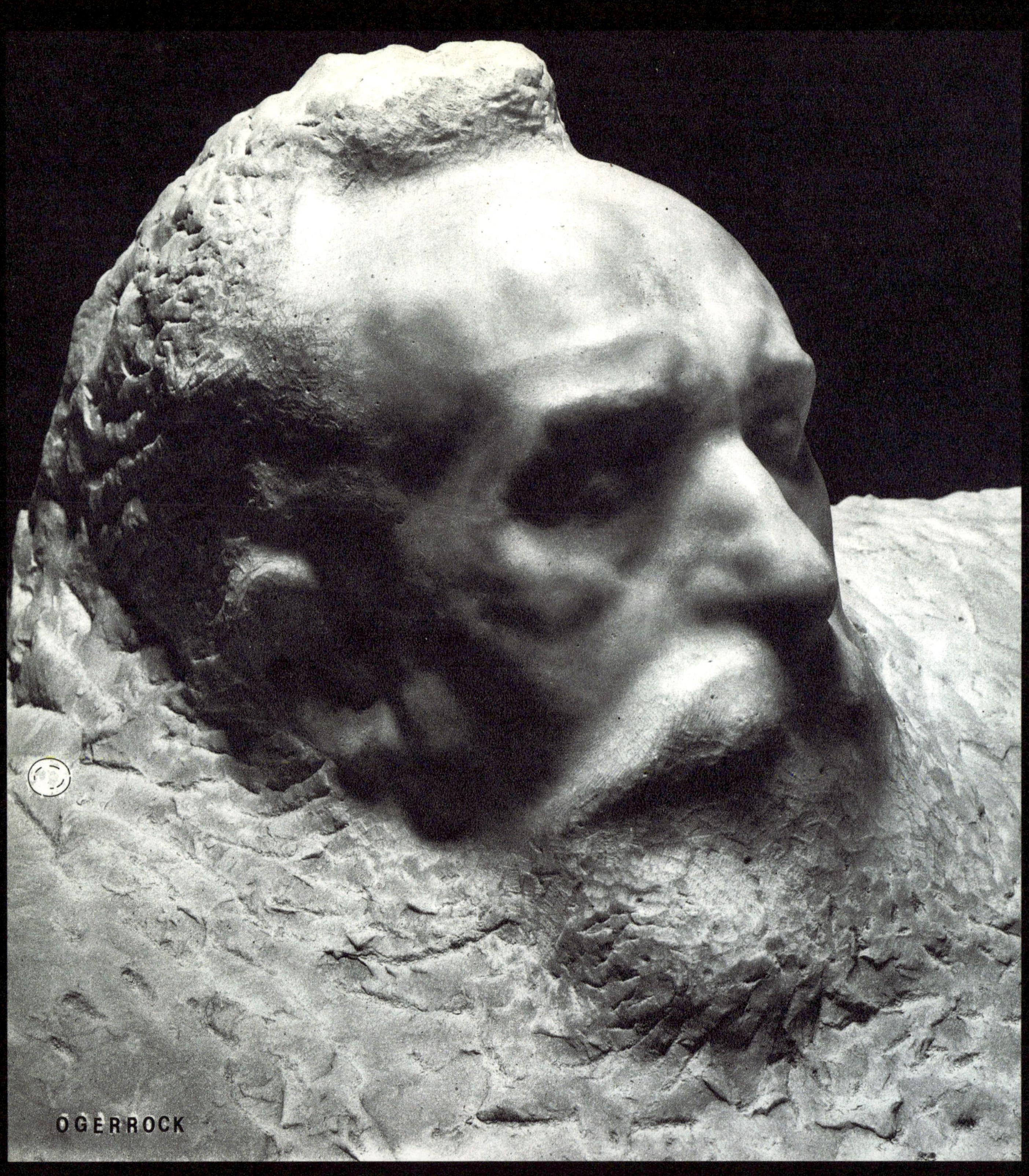
OGERROCK

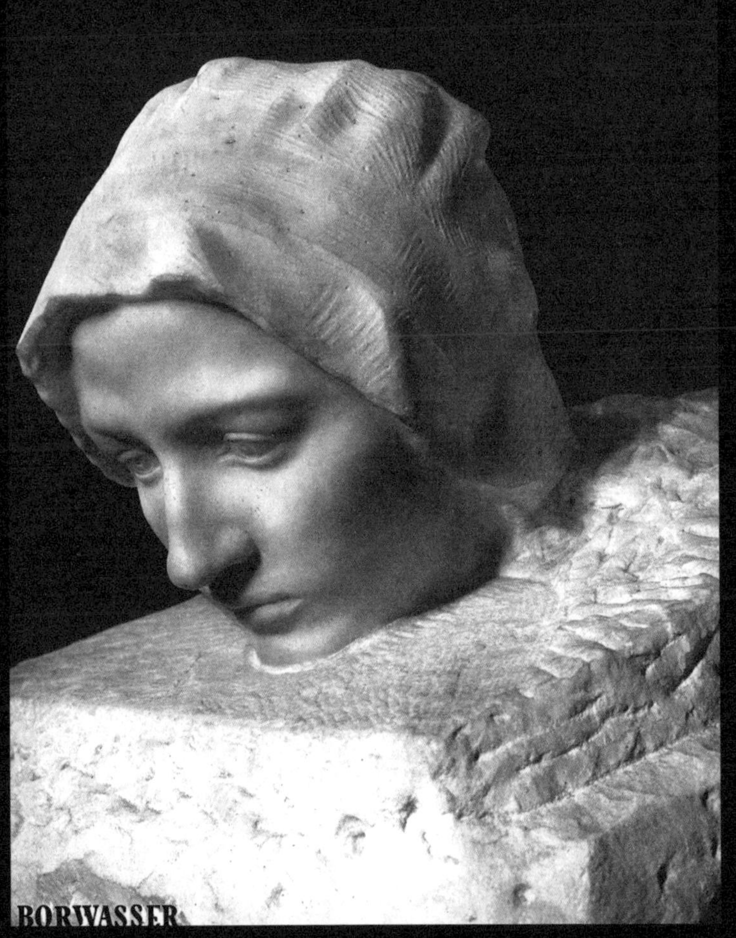
BORWASSER

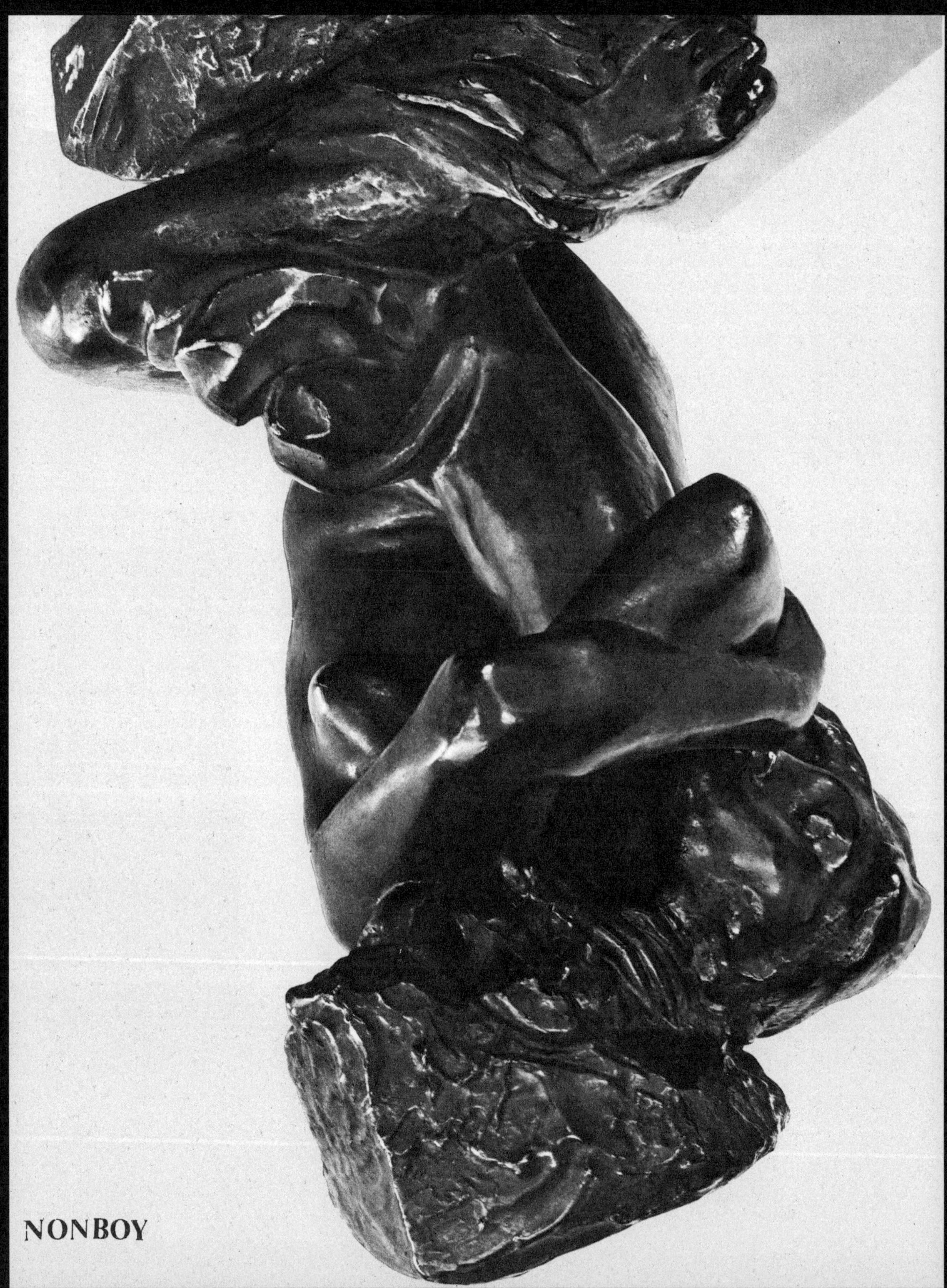
NONBOY

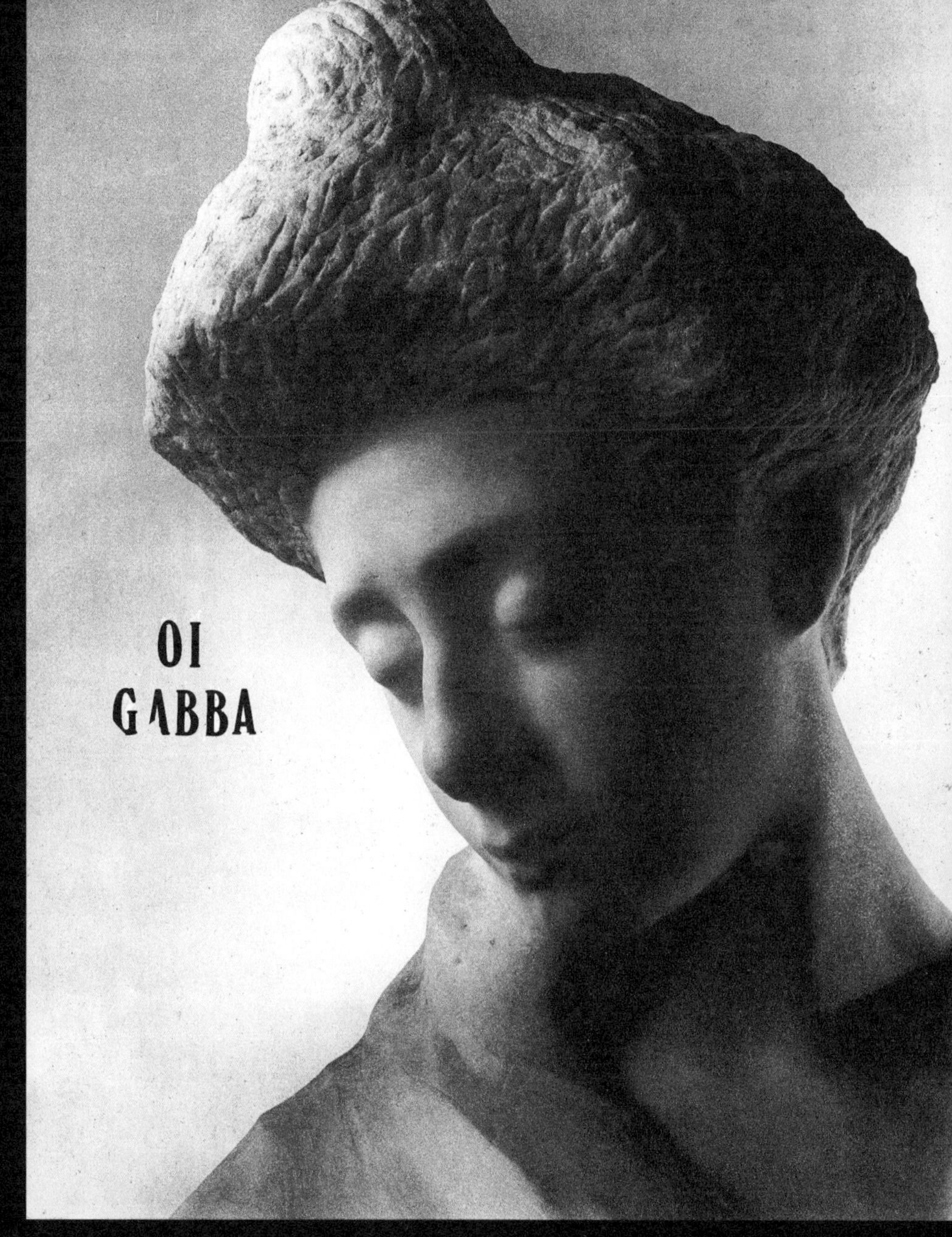

OI
GABBA

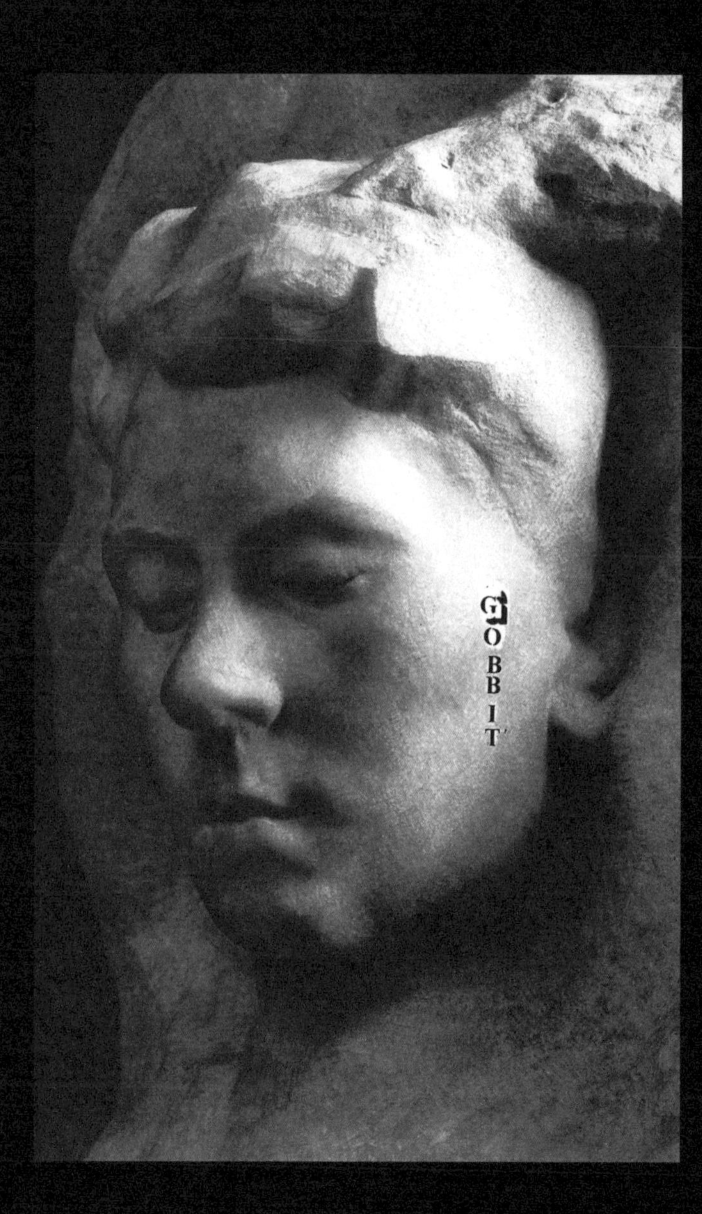
GOBBIT

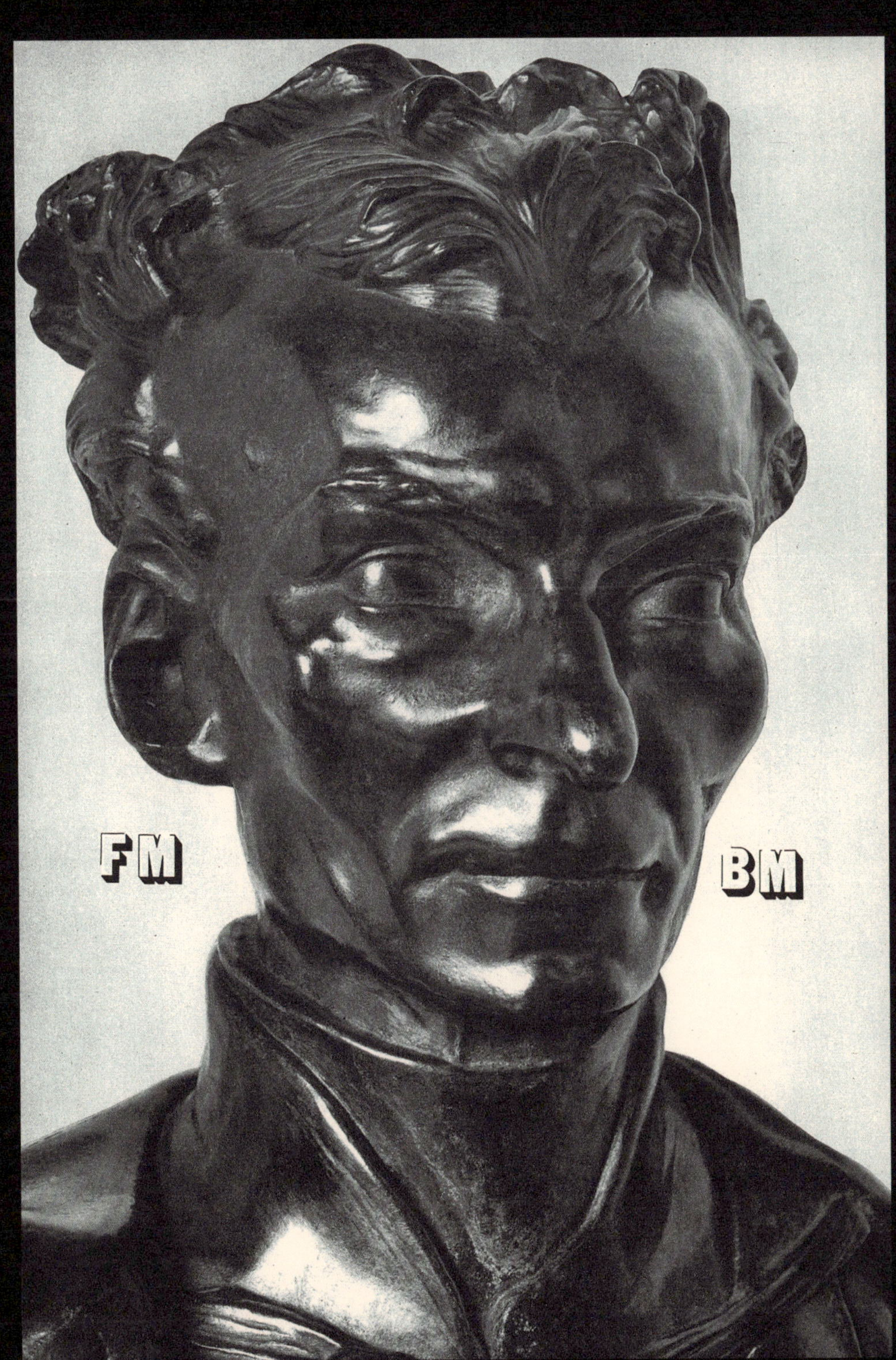

FM
BM

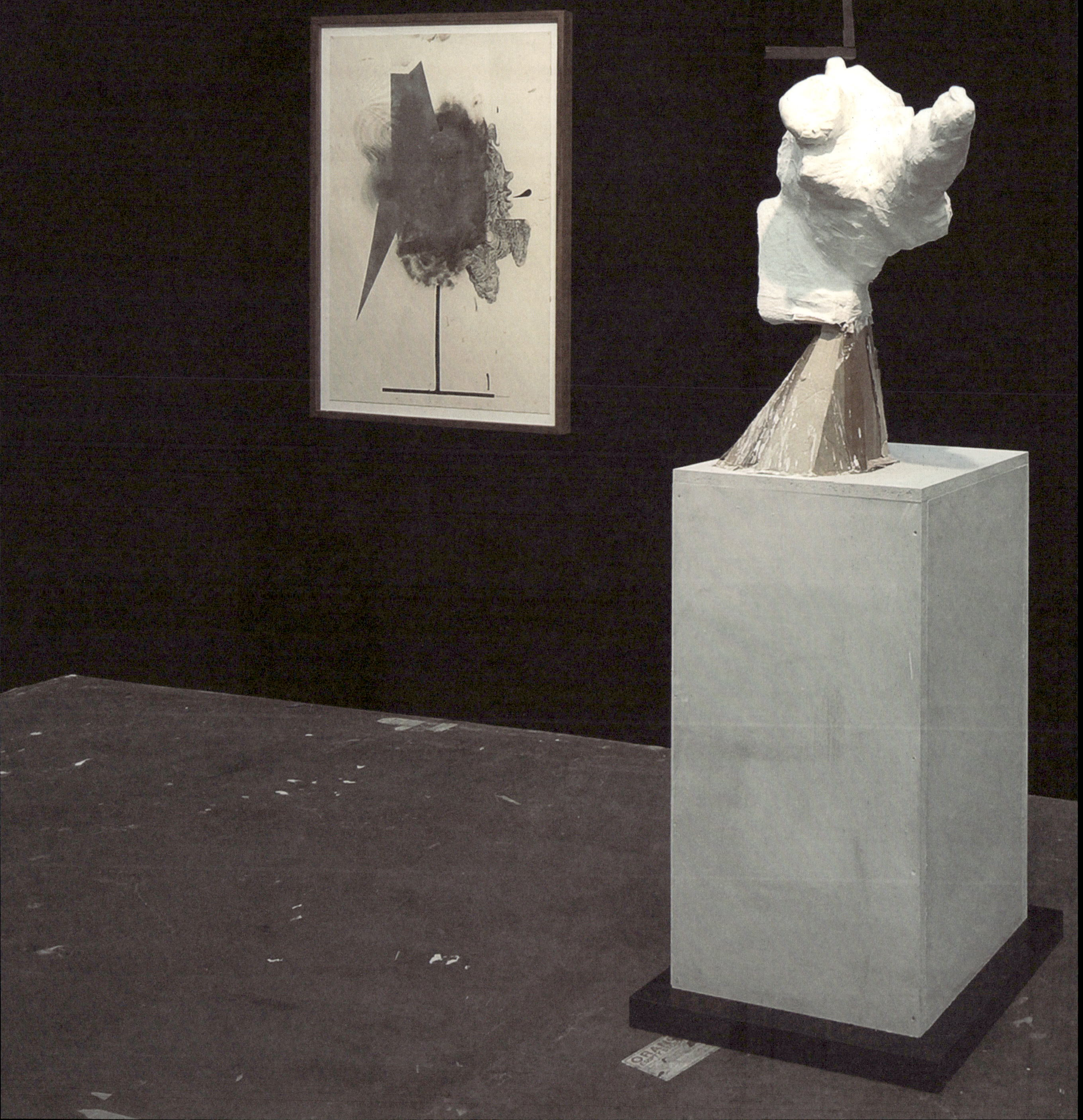

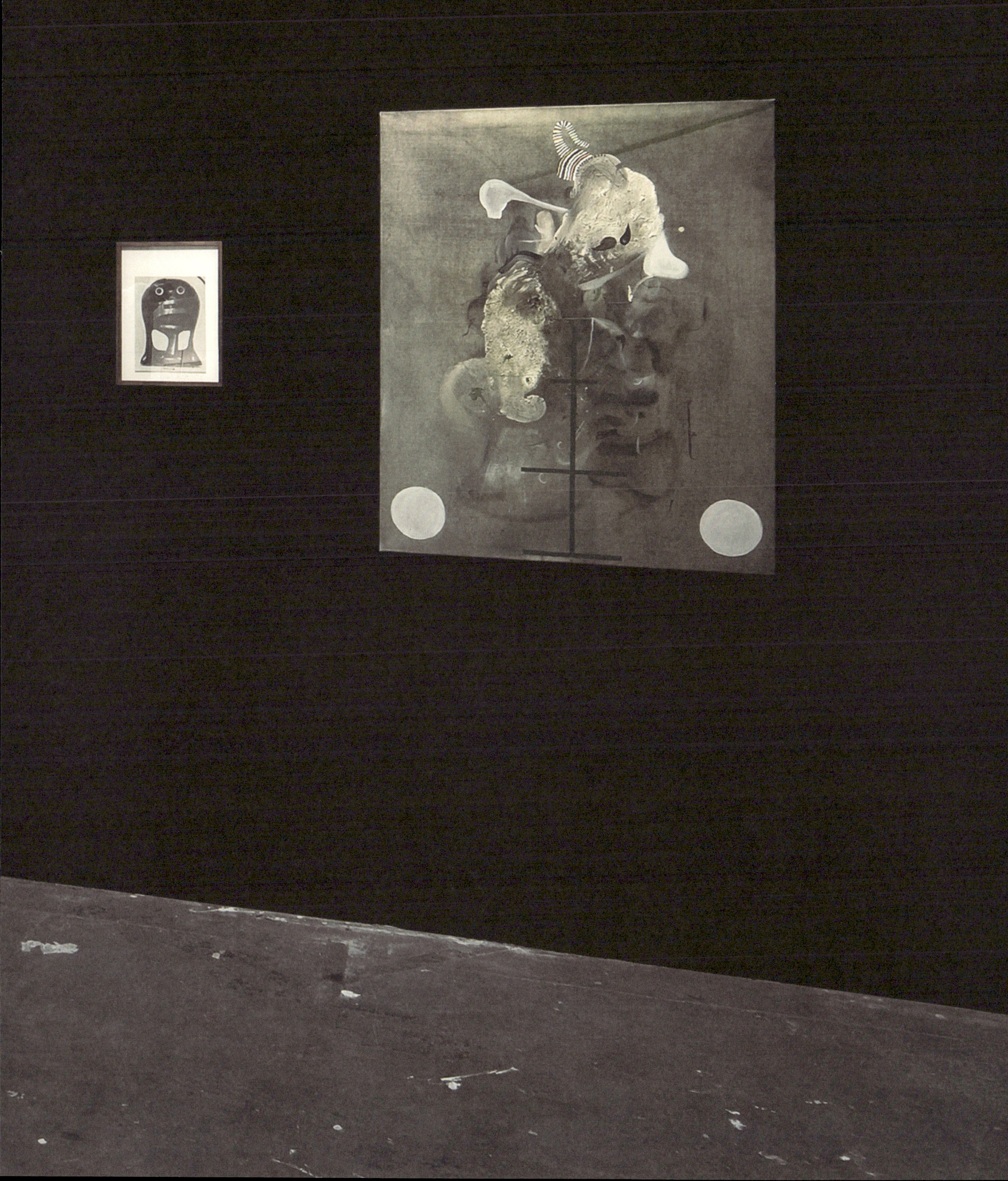

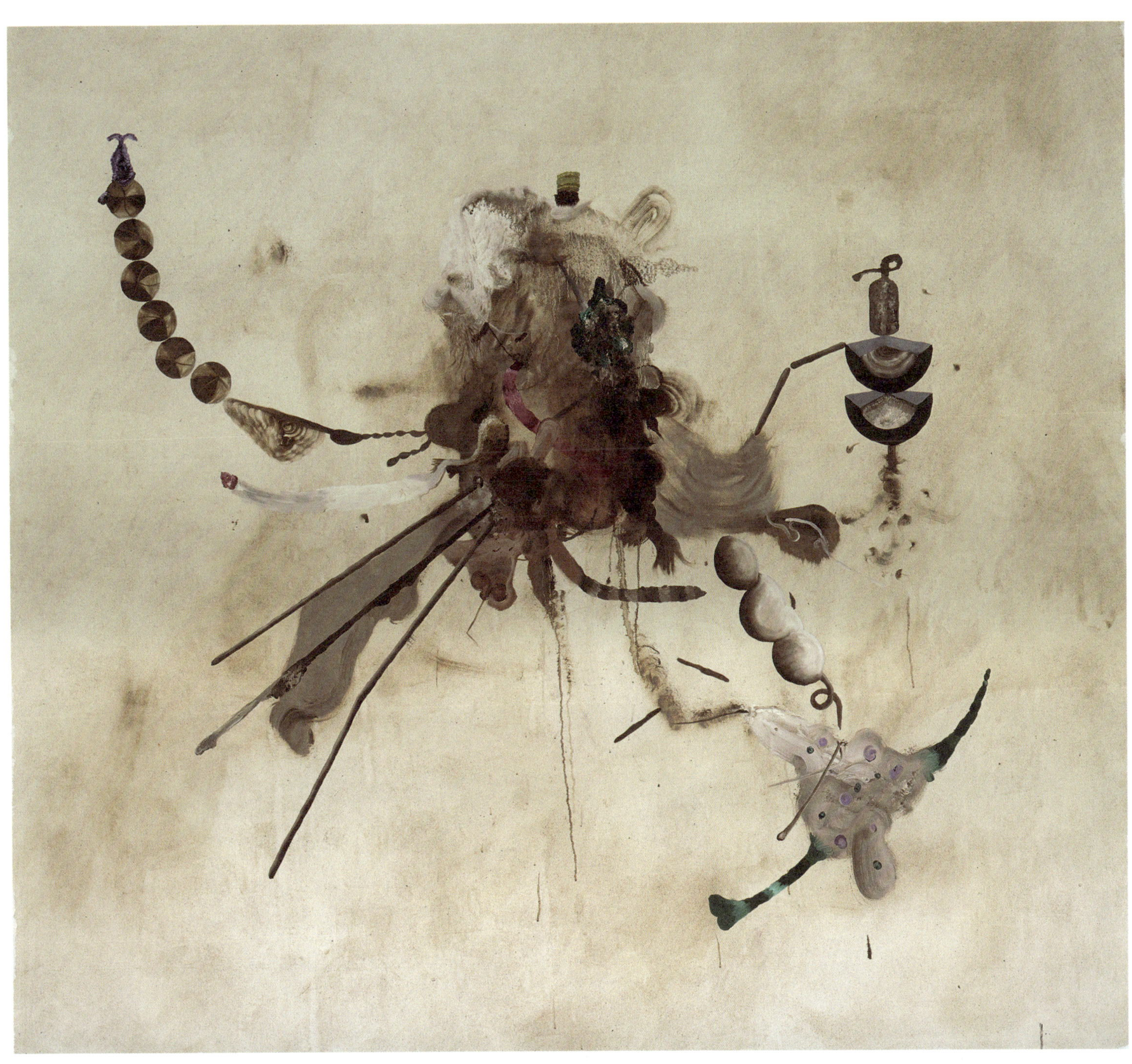

L.O.R.D.S. 7000 (der neue Haw-Haw), 2006, oil on canvas, 190 x 210 cm

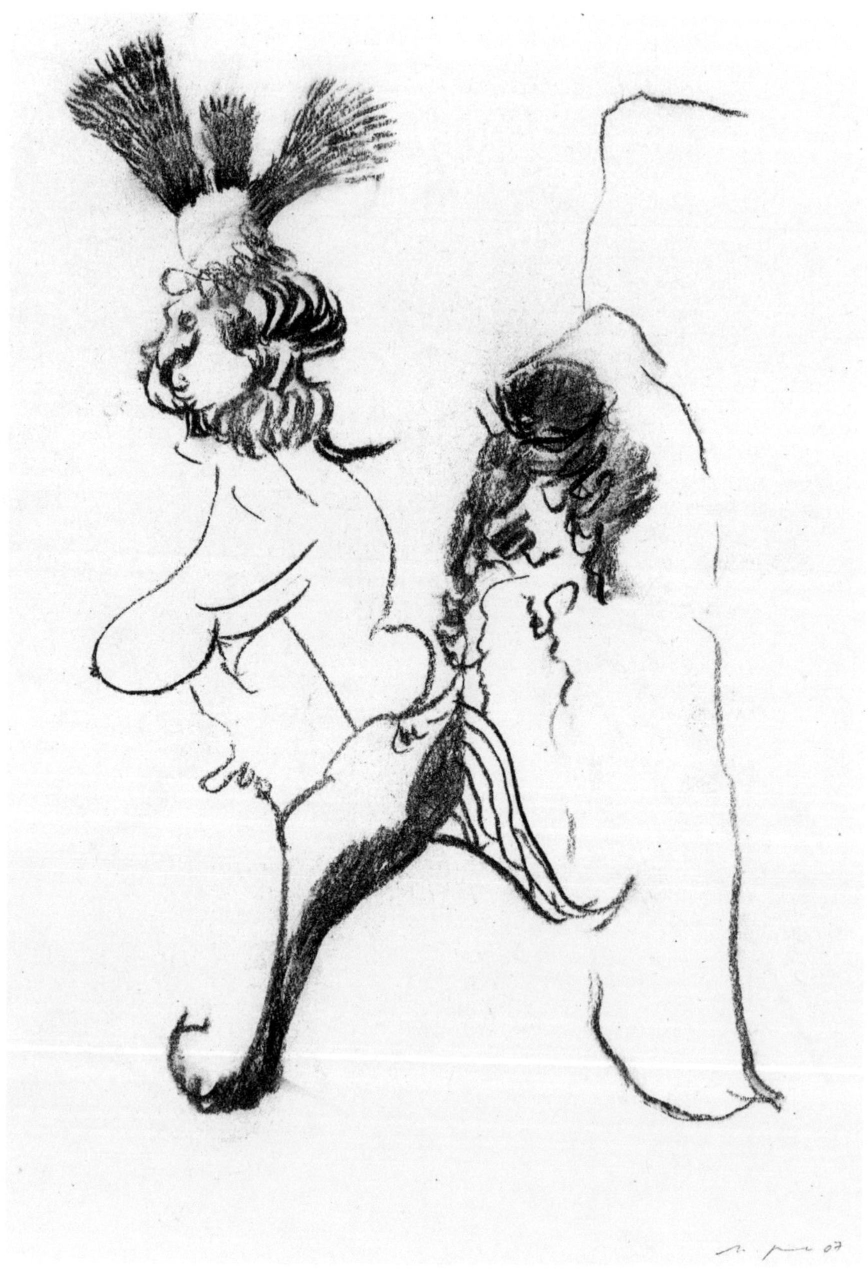

Untitled, 2007, charcoal on paper, 29.7 x 21 cm

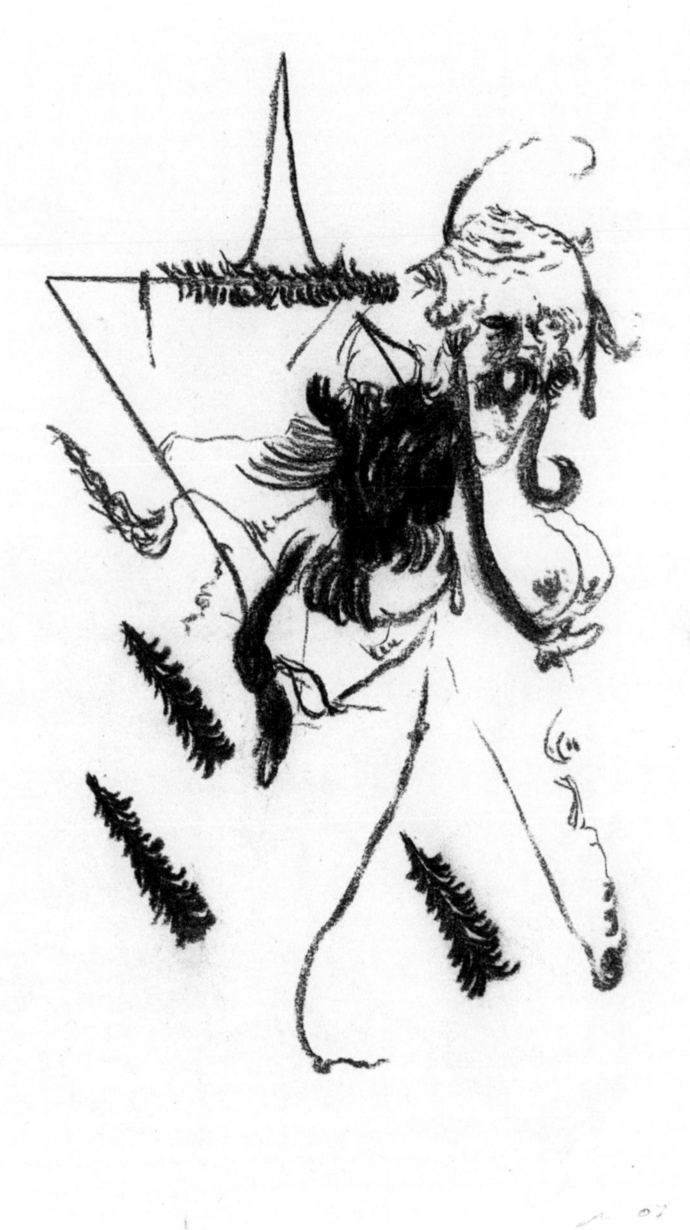

Empe Gibson, 2007, charcoal on paper, 29.7 x 21 cm

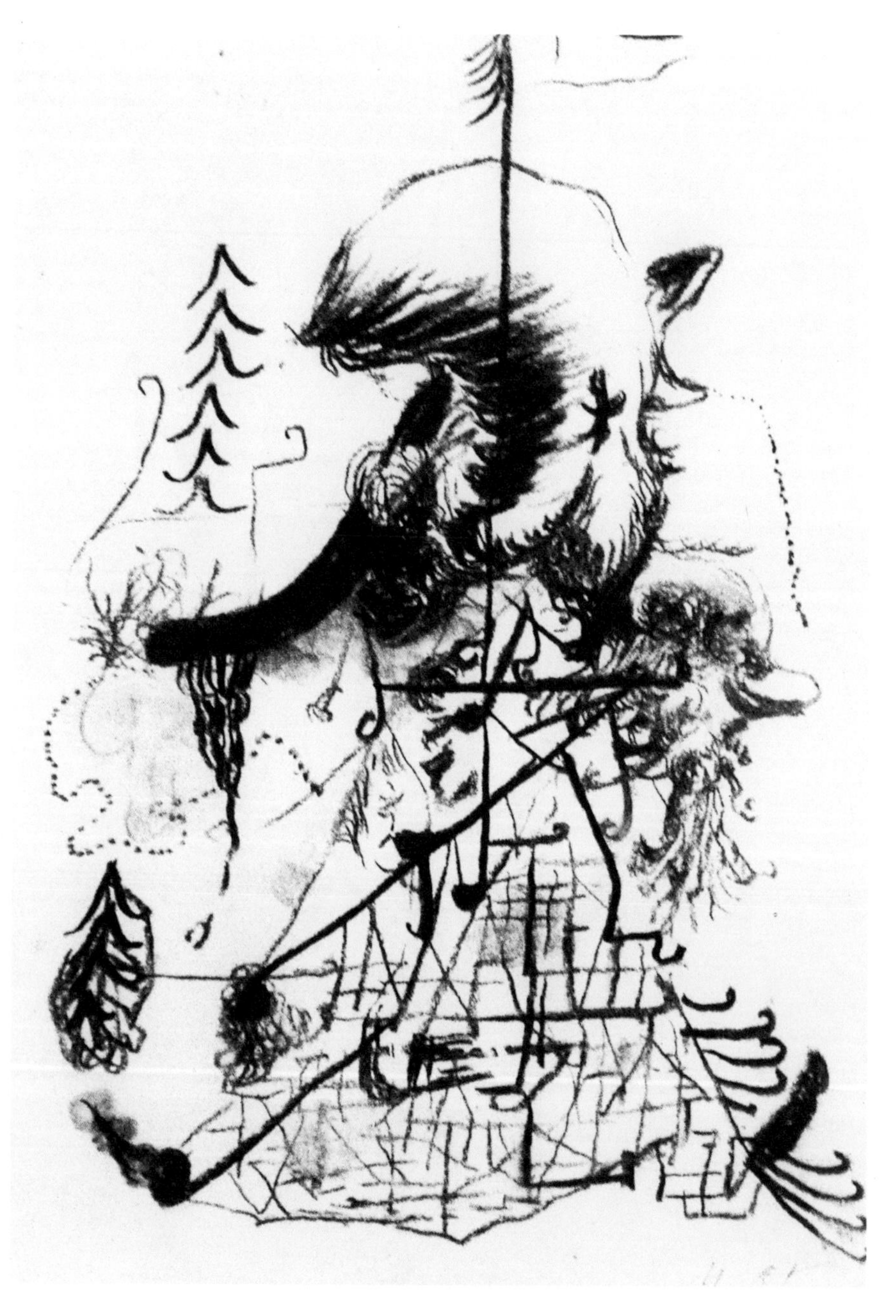

Charriot, 2007, charcoal on paper, 29.7 x 21 cm

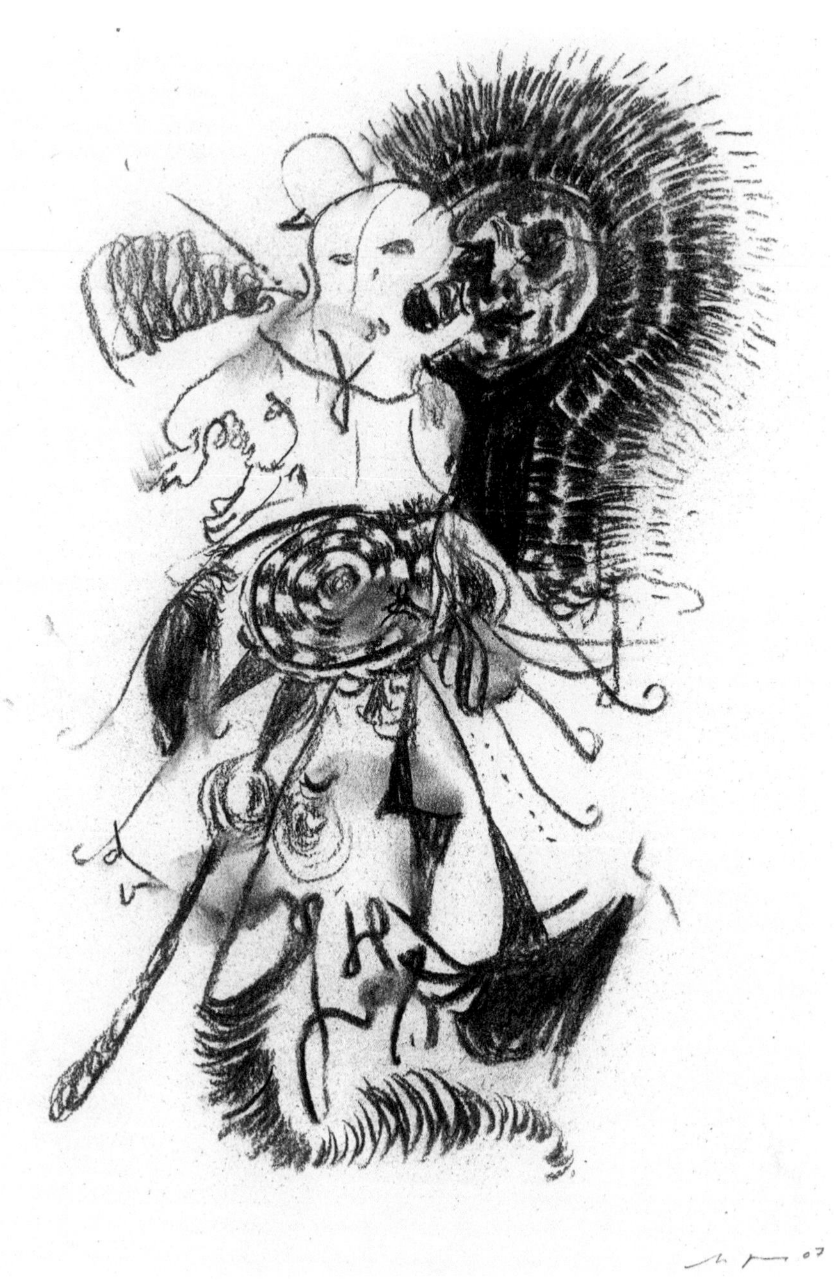

Untitled, 2007, charcoal on paper, 29.7 x 21 cm

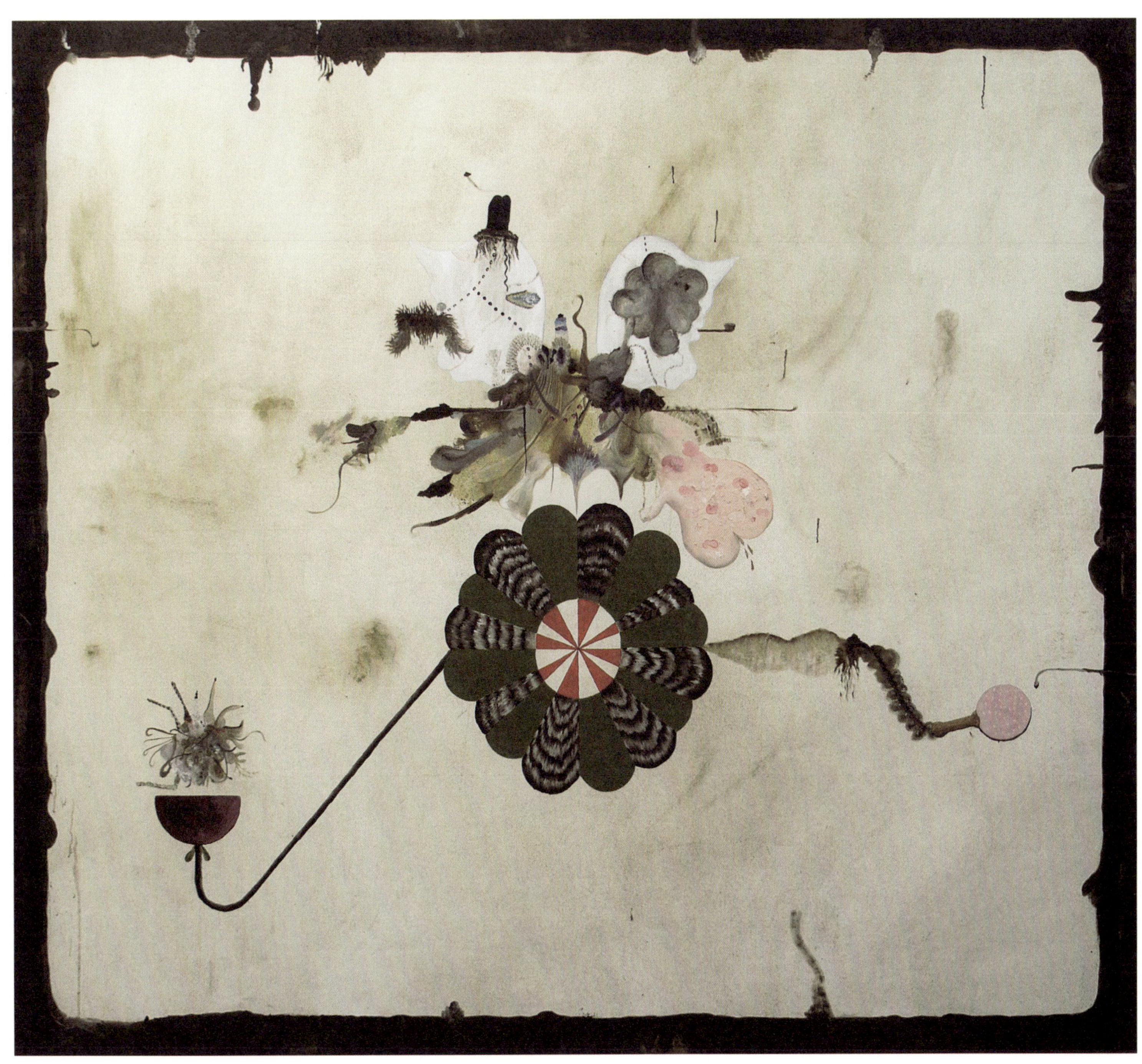

L.O.R.D.S. 3000, 2006, oil on canvas, 190 x 210 cm

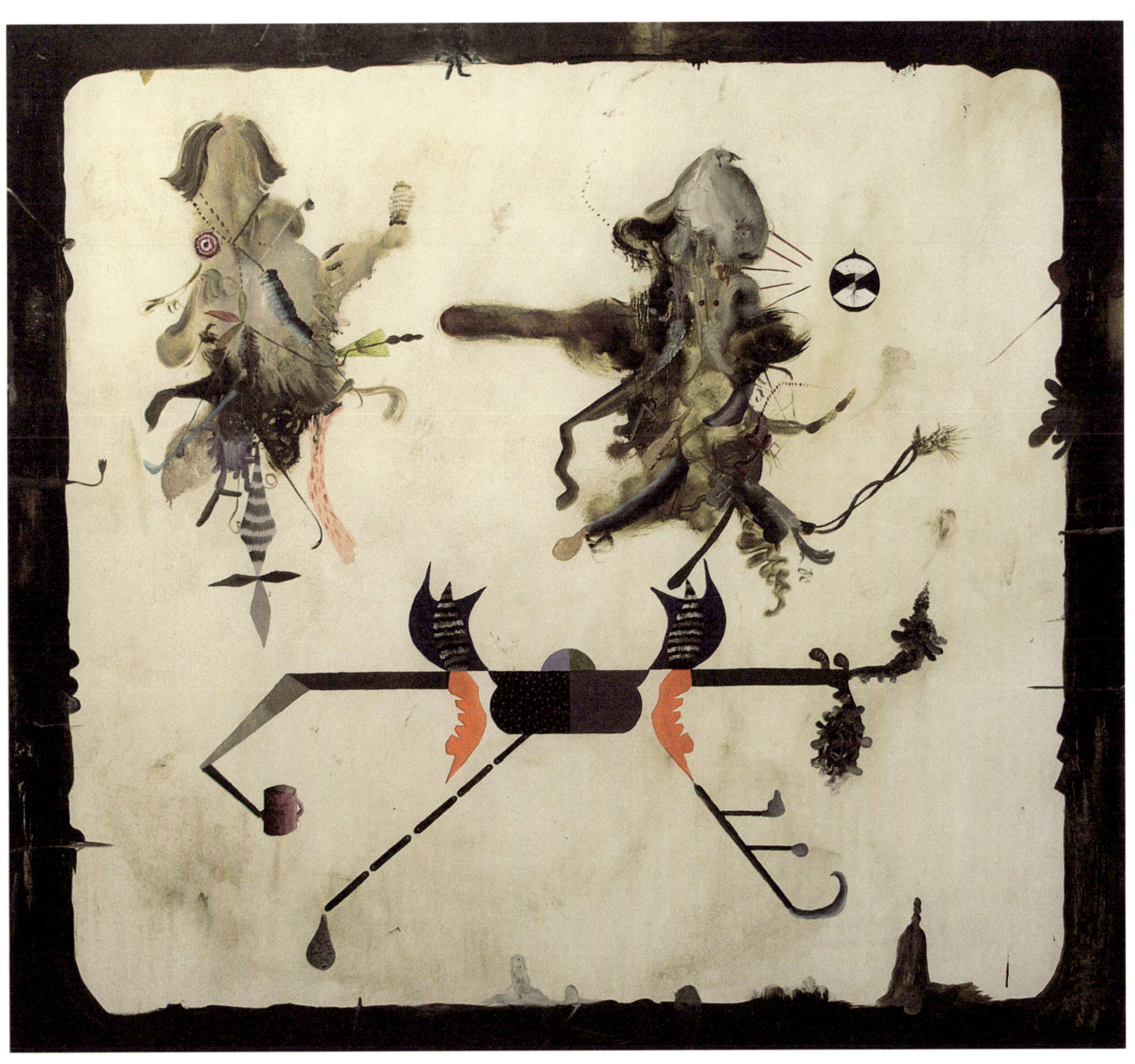

L.O.R.D.S. 4000, 2006, oil on canvas, 190 x 210 cm

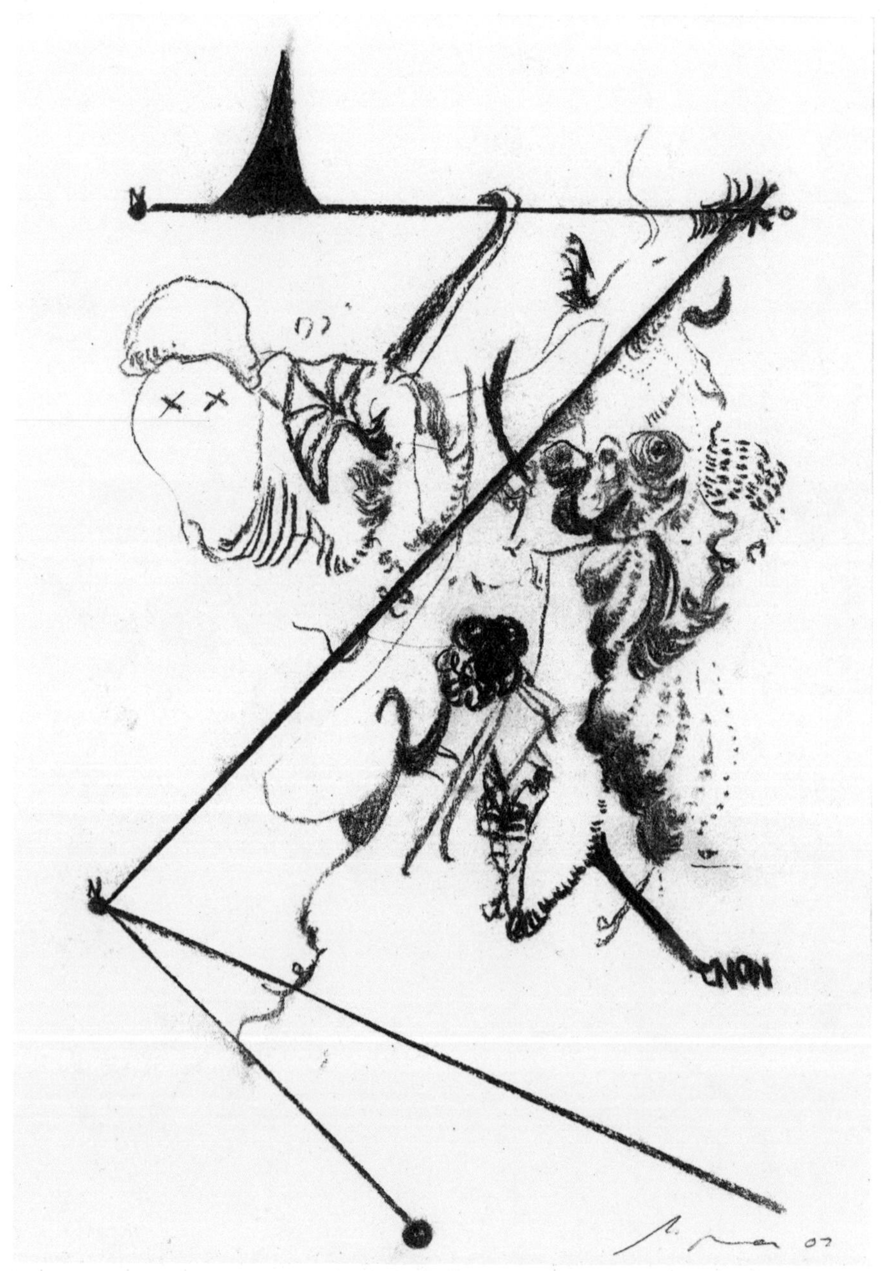

Doof Gallery, 2007, charcoal on paper, 29.7 x 21 cm

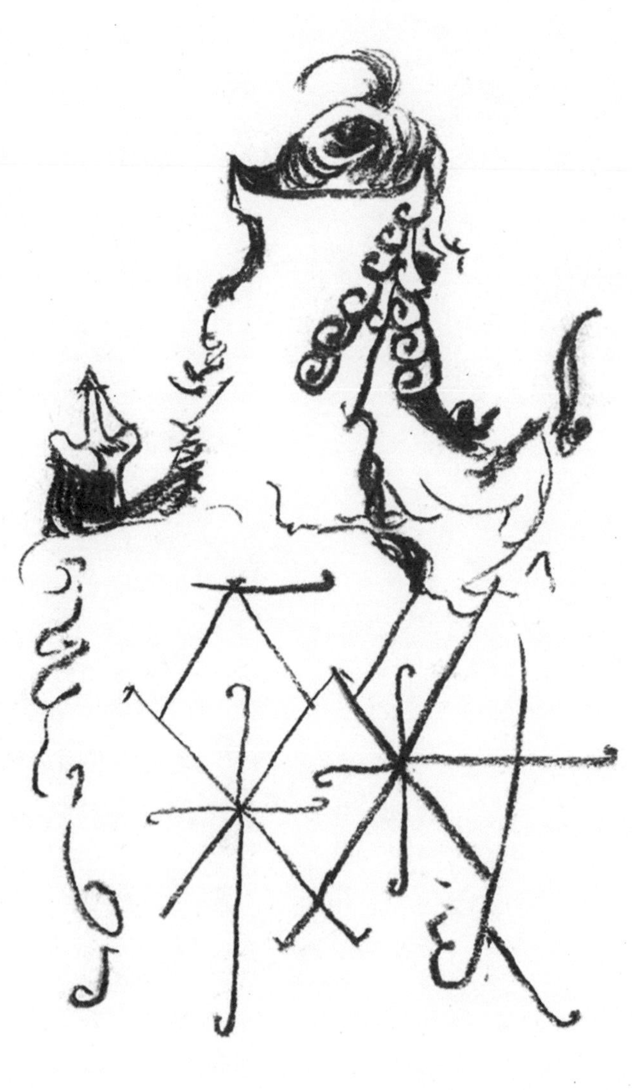

Untitled, 2007, charcoal on paper, 29.7 x 21 cm

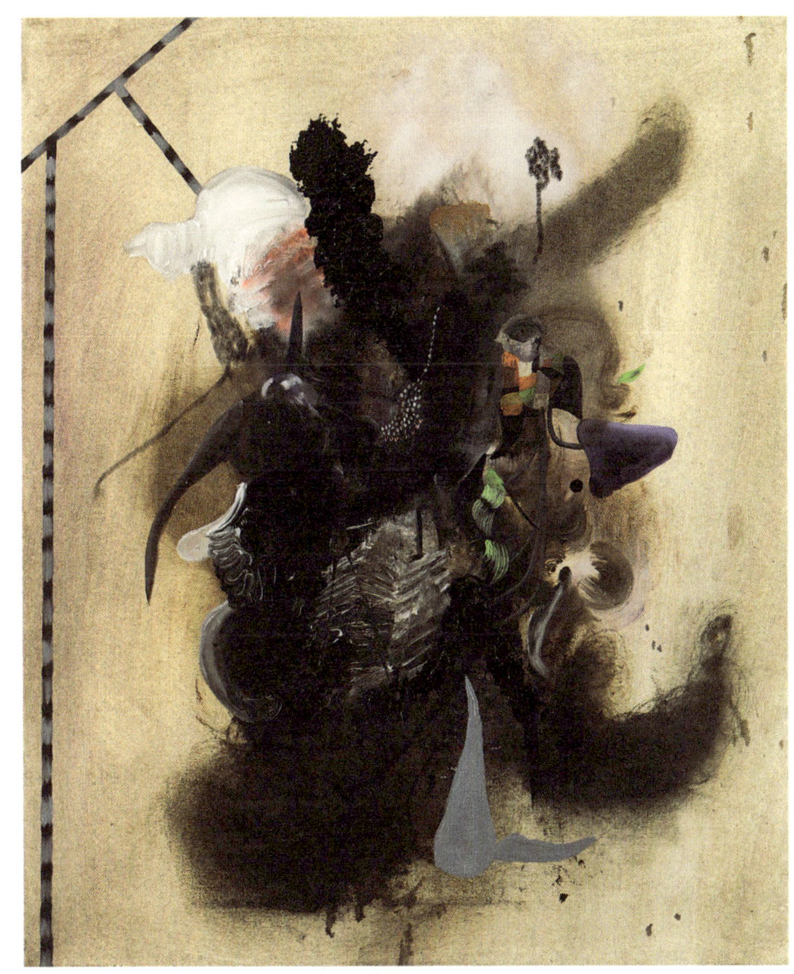

SUBSTITUTE 3, 2007, oil on canvas, 60 x 50 cm

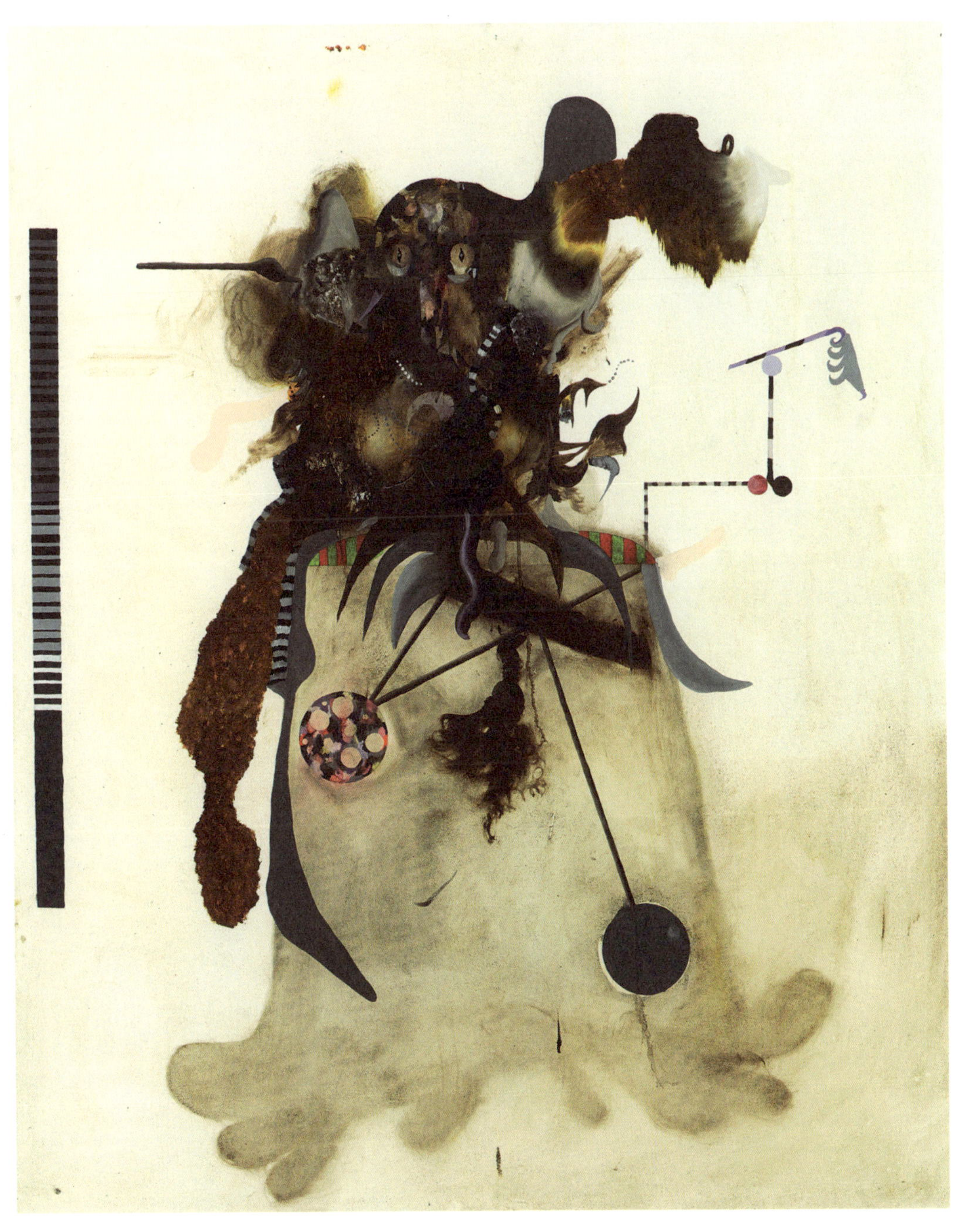

B/M–YLMAZ–UHOS, 2007, oil on canvas, 160 x 130 cm

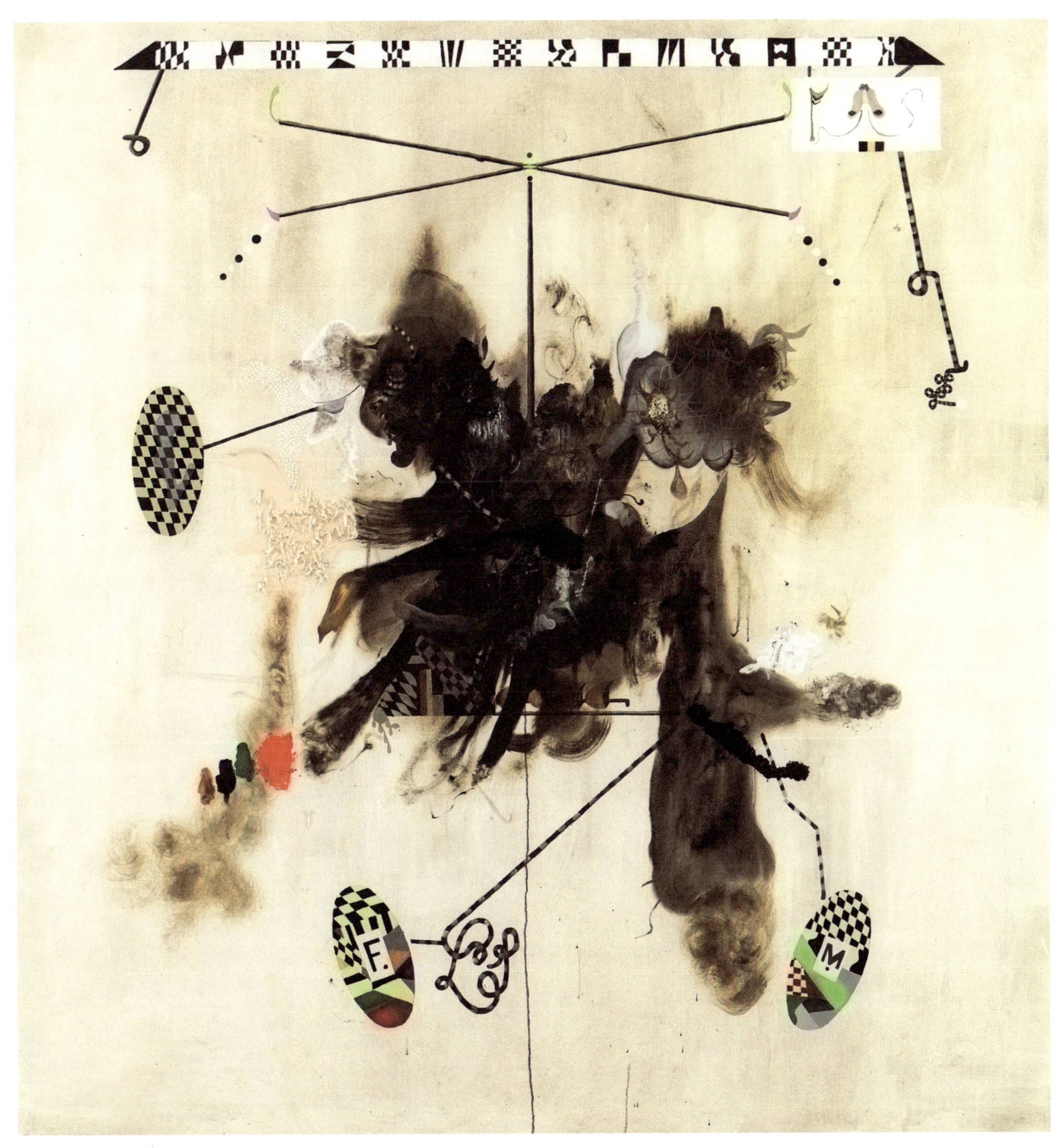

F/M–B/M 80 Million Years, 2007, oil on canvas, 200 x 190 cm

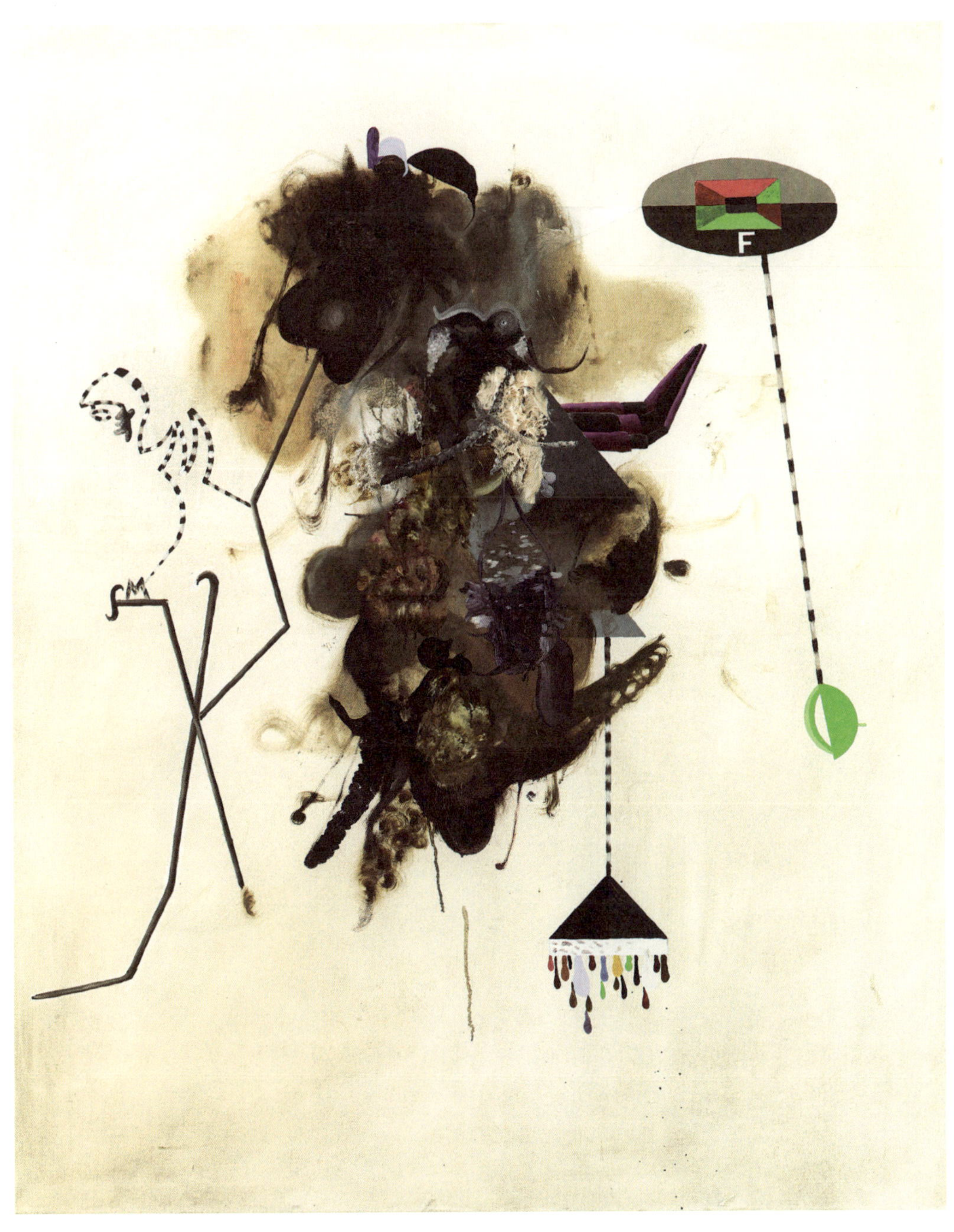

B/M–B–Magneta, 2007, oil on canvas, 160 x 130 cm

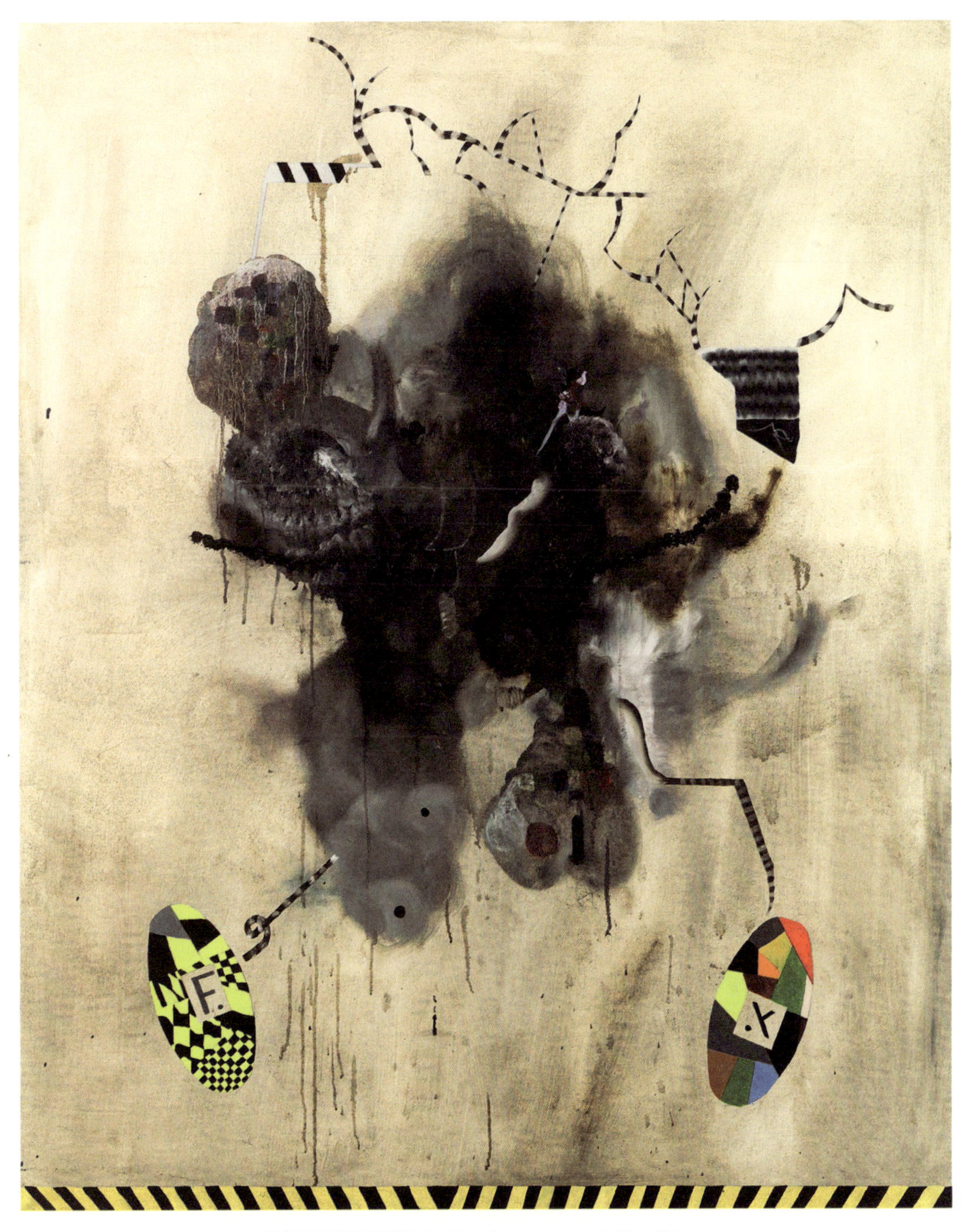

F/M SVORBEN, 2007, oil on canvas, 160 x 130 cm

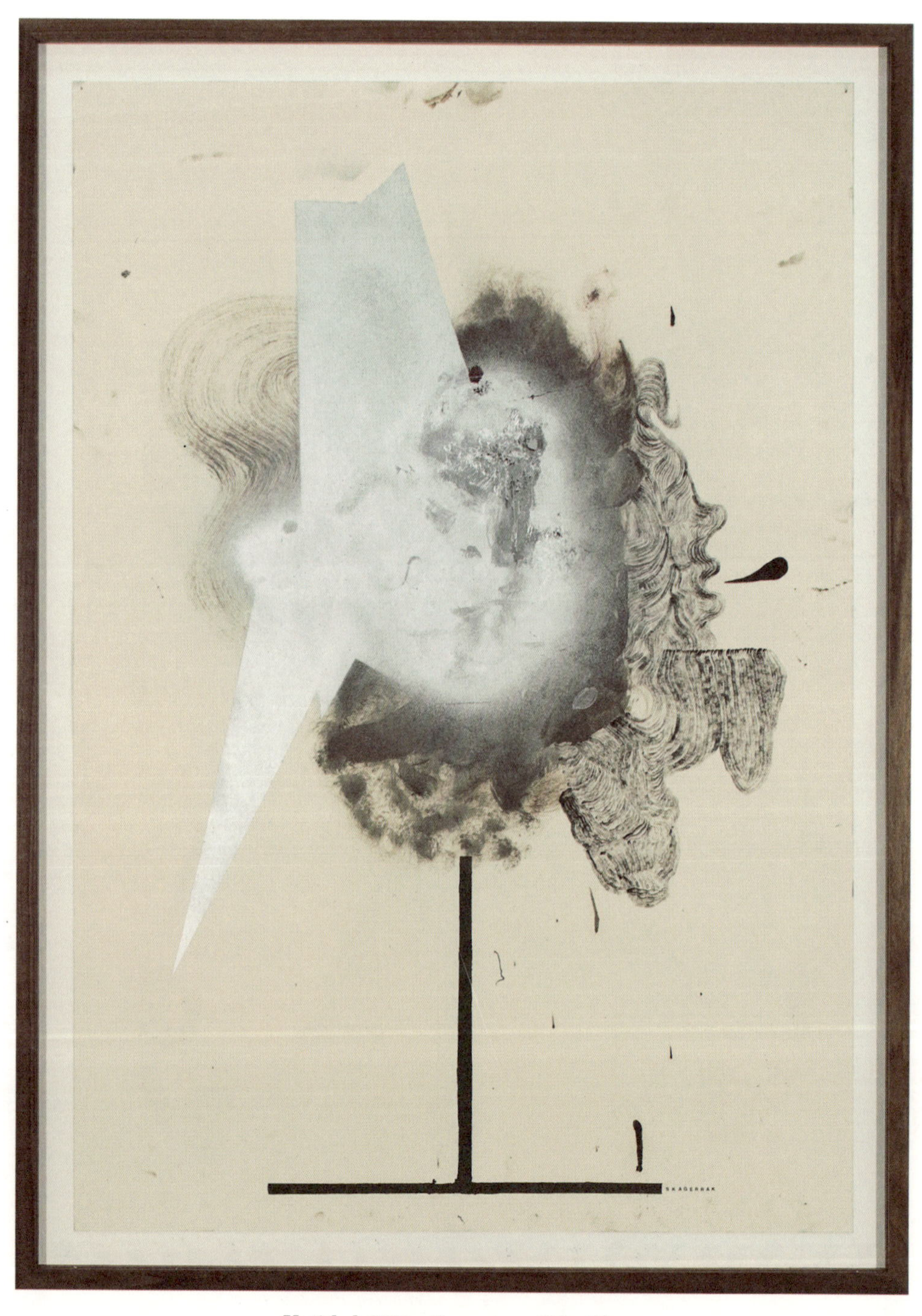

Untitled, 2008, oil on paper, 100 x 70 cm

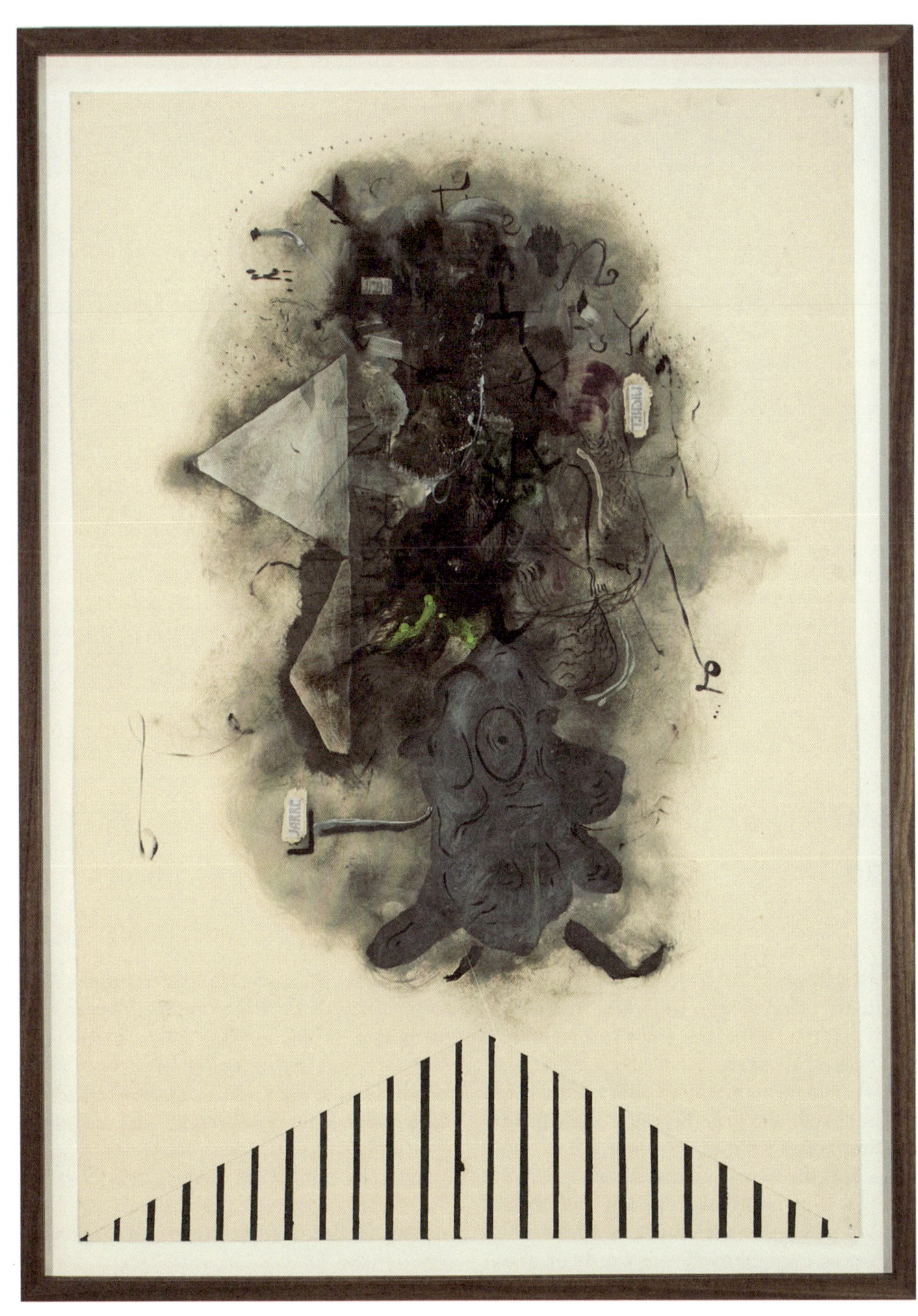

Untitled, 2008, oil on paper, 100 x 70 cm

Begin Again

Jennifer Higgie

In Michael Bauer's paintings tendrils ascend, wilt and dissolve in a sepia gloom; occasionally they float, enmeshed in eyeballs or ribbons of bright, rich color that rises from the wreckage of a tough geometry. These are images partly built from non-sequiturs, flamboyant shards of bodies, and spiky, fabricated animals—they're fragmented, sexual, feverish and funny; worlds within worlds that won't be pinned down. They make me think of filthy cities, and filthier minds; of lavish interiors, abandoned excavations, half-remembered rituals, snatches of music and inexplicable joy. The paint breathes and spawns like mud, and, like mud, it encourages growth—of words or unexpected detours into humor or allusions to a mythology of lost codes. But there is also something of the bird about these pictures, in their beaky protrusions, feathery, jewel-like flashes of color and light, flights of fancy.

As much as modernity has attempted to argue for reason and linearity, perception—and, by association, most people's

In Michael Bauers Malerei winden sich Ranken empor, sie welken dahin und lösen sich in sepiafarbener Düsternis auf; bisweilen schweben sie auch, verwoben in Augäpfeln oder Bändern aus leuchtender, schwerer Farbe, die sich aus den Trümmern einer spannungsreichen Geometrie erheben. Hier haben wir es mit Bildern zu tun, die sich teilweise aus visuellen Gedankensprüngen, grossgestischen Körperscherben und stachligen, künstlich gefertigten Tieren formen – sie wirken fragmentiert, sexuell, fiebrig und lustig; Welten in Welten, die sich dem Zugriff entziehen. Mich lassen sie an schmutzige Städte und an noch schmutzigere Seelen denken; an verschwenderische Interieurs, zurückgelassene Ausgrabungsstätte, kaum erinnerte Rituale, Musikfetzen und unerklärliche Freude. Die Farbe atmet und erzeugt Neues wie Schlamm, und sie begünstigt, darin ebenfalls mit Schlamm vergleichbar, Wachstumsprozesse – von Worten oder unerwarteten Abschweifungen ins Humoreske oder in Anspielungen auf eine

relationship to sight—has never discarded its innate state of disarray (we see what we want to see, despite evidence to the contrary, and then translate it accordingly). Nothing can ever be truly whole, complete or resolved when we live in an infinite state of flux—how could it be, when everything will change in the blink of an eye? (Sometimes when you have just woken up, the world appears made of fragments. Before your eyes it gradually reassembles itself.) Thus, in a beautiful paradox, paintings, drawings and sculptures that resist singular readings, and that are, by their very nature, cautious in their refusal to ascribe intention, can be curiously more representative of our thought processes than work that proclaims its meaning in water-tight phrases of accountability. (We look too quickly, we think incompletely, and we follow very little through.) Given how much we all live in our heads—and how much of our lives we spend sleeping, dreaming and daydreaming, alone with our thoughts—it could be said that Bauer's imaginary world, as full as it is of phantasms, inventions, atmospherics and hallucinations, describes reality more accurately than any photograph; after all, sight is as subjective and temporal as it is natural, physical and unmediated. Our various worlds, his images seem to be saying, are built from shards of meaning, some knowledge, slivers of instinct, and a lot of intuition.

The relationship to time in Bauer's work is slippery. Like a twisted history of the 20th century, symbols and psychoanalysis tangle with everyday detritus: mathematics, eyeballs, circles and cigarettes, hints of harlequins, elaborate phalluses and plump orifices, psychedelic patterns and the murmur of unspecified music. Suggestions of 18th century portraits and 20th century cartoons, in loony smudges or strange figures formed from amalgamations of myriad objects and shapes, loom from hazy atmospheres, like characters in an elaborate joke, the punch-line of which is never revealed. Words offer little illumination here: titles function more like tiny, enigmatic poems than as aides to reason. In the painting *B / M – Ylmaz – Uhos*, 2007 (a particularly inscrutable title that casts no light whatsoever on its subject), what appears to be a small, rotund figure with bulging, varnished cheeks and staring, displaced owl's eyes, morphs into a playful mobile of swinging balls, and deep smoky tarnish, while a long, striped and somber bar to the left of the central image recalls supermarket pricing codes.

Bauer's paintings seem more comfortable with shadows and half-light: I imagine them blooming in twilight, or early morning, or settling in gloomy, overcast afternoons, when gray skies intensify the depth of colors. Sepia, with all its connotations of death, decay and memory, shimmers like a thin veneer over many of these pictures. In *Pol 1 (Smart Estrus)*, 2005, for example, a severed head is formed from fleshy protrusions, beads and a single staring eye—as if nothing could be worse than the inability to see. Canvases are littered with vicious, even grotesque figures and sudden shifts in tone: holes (as if nothing is water-tight), patches of murky green, and strange, pinkish, grayish skin drift above a bright, patterned banner. A neat, black and white feather sprouts from this being's head. For all its innate surrealism, however, it's a solemn, weirdly dignified, portrait; like a homage to a long-dead aristocrat painted for a family in the future, it declares its mystery without apology. Similarly,

Mythologie verlorener Codes. Doch haben diese Bilder auch etwas Vogelgleiches, in ihren schnabelförmigen Vorsprüngen, in den fedrigen, juwelenartigen Farb- und Lichtblitzen, den Höhenflügen ihrer Fantasie.

So sehr auch die Moderne für Rationalität und Linearität einzutreten versucht haben mag, die Wahrnehmung – und damit auch die Beziehung, die die meisten zur ihrem Sehvermögen unterhalten – hat den ihr innewohnenden Verwirrungszustand nie verlassen (wir sehen, was wir sehen wollen, wider besseren Wissens, und passen es dann entsprechend an). Nichts kann jemals wahrhaft ganz, vollendet oder aufgelöst sein, wenn wir uns doch in einem unendlichen Flusszustand befinden – wie sollte es das auch sein, wenn sich doch alles noch im Augenblick verändern wird? (Manchmal gleich nach dem Aufwachen erscheint die Welt wie in Bruchstücken. Vor unseren Augen fügt sie sich dann nach und nach zusammen.) In dieser Weise können Gemälde, Zeichnungen und Skulpturen, die sich einfacher Lektüre entziehen und die ihrer eigensten Natur gemäss bei der Zuschreibung einer Intention Vorsicht walten lassen, auf seltsame Weise unsere Denkvorgänge besser repräsentieren als solche Werke, die ihre Bedeutung im wasserdichten Phrasen der Zurechnungsfähigkeit vor sich her tragen. (Wir schauen zu flüchtig hin, wir schliessen unsere Gedankengänge nicht ab, lassen überhaupt bei wenigen Dingen Konsequenz walten.) Berücksichtigt man das hohe Mass, in dem wir alle in unseren Köpfen leben – und welch grosse Anteile unseres Lebens wir schlafend, träumend, tagträumend verbringen –, dann könnte man sagen, dass Bauers imaginäre Welt, so sehr sie auch vor Fantasmen, Erfindungen, Stimmungen und Sinnestäuschungen strotzt, die Wirklichkeit präziser zu beschreiben vermag als jede Fotografie; denn schliesslich ist alles Sehen ebenso subjektiv und an Zeit gebunden wie es natürlich, physisch und unvermittelt ist. Unsere verschiedenen Welten – das scheinen seine Bilder sagen zu wollen – bestehen aus Bedeutungsscherben, ein wenig Wissen, ein paar Instinktsplittern und einer Menge Intuition.

Das Verhältnis zum Zeitlichen, das sich in Bauers Werk findet, ist schwer zu fassen. Wie in einer verdrehten Geschichte des 20. Jahrhunderts vermischen sich Symbole und Psychoanalytisches mit dem Gerümpel des Alltags: Mathematik, Augäpfel, Kreise und Zigaretten, angedeutete Harlekine, sorgfältig ausgeführte Phalli und pralle Körperöffnungen, psychedelische Muster und das Gemurmel nicht näher bestimmbarer Musik. Andeutungen von Porträts aus dem 18. und Cartoons aus dem 20. Jahrhundert zeichnen sich in verrückten Schmierern oder merkwürdigen Figuren in trüben Atmosphären ab, die sich aus der Zusammenklumpung von Myriaden von Objekten und Formen gebildet haben, wie Figuren in einem aufwändigen Witz, dessen Pointe man nie erfährt. Worte haben hier wenig Erhellendes beizutragen: die Bildtitel funktionieren eher wie winzige, verrätselte Gedichte denn als Stützen der Erkenntnis. In dem Gemälde B/M – Ylmaz – Uhos (2007) – dieser Titel ist ganz besonders undurchsichtig und erlaubt keinerlei Rückschluss auf irgendeinen Inhalt – morpht eine klein und kugelig scheinende Figur mit vorgewölbten Wangen und starrenden, eigenartig platzierten Eulenaugen zu einem verspielten Mobile aus schaukelnden Bällen und einem tiefen, rauchigen Überzug, während ein langer, gestreifter

Pol 3 (Kamerad Säckle), 2005,—a painting of the floating head of a deer-like animal with a bright eyeball, surrounded by what I can only describe as a kind of milky ectoplasm, hovering above a single, pink teardrop—looks like a time traveler; but whether from the past or future, it's hard to say.

Where the charcoal drawings are fluent, fast and uncorrected—like compositions hard-wired straight from the brain, Bauer uses oil paint to struggle with an idea, to stain and bruise it as its shape emerges. As a result, the surfaces of these paintings are richly textured—swathes of loose and dreamy washes are rammed against chalky globules of pigment, or tough graphic lines. Look closely and signs of a tussle become apparent in the flushed pinks, bloody reds and battered ochers that wrestle with the peachy browns, and in the choppy areas of paint that bleed over soft ground marked by acid greens and dark lines as delicate as hair. Often a sense of lightness floats up unexpectedly from the gluey mud. For example, in a recent, opulently layered painting, *Bad Harvest*, 2008, the loose delineation of a figure materializes from an earthy ground, built from thick, almost sculptural sections of dirty white paint that are juxtaposed with shapes rendered with great elegance: two soft, golden globes swing in space like Christmas baubles, while an elegant geometric arm balances what looks like a pottery shard; a tiny bird with a purple head hangs suspended from a kind of feathery beak above zebra-like patterning, and a line of color along the bottom of the picture recalls tribal rugs. Inexplicably, a neat, deep green line runs diagonally across the painting, from the top right corner to the bottom left. While the title of the picture alludes to something ominous, its composition and feverish imagination create an atmosphere of spooky mythology—as if something compelling and possibly sinister might lie just beyond our comprehension.

Bauer's monochromatic and abstract sculptures hit a different note to the paintings and stand before them like anthropomorphic sentinels on plain, even flimsy supports. Often counter-intuitive, they are large, lush, a little inscrutable and full of personality. Although their features are indeterminate, it's impossible not to read their ample contours as genial phalluses or noses rising from chunky, soulful heads (why they seem a little sad, even heartbreaking, is beyond me). They melt, droop, attempt to stand to attention or stare straight ahead, their skins formed from tough, often shiny materials—glass tiles, or plaster of paris finished in high-gloss black, bright white, deep purple, or lime green. Like thoughts made flesh, the sculptures are occasionally adorned with ordinary objects from everyday life, including rice cakes, nicotine patches, a pen or pills in resin. These are sculptures that lend themselves to make-believe. I would swear, for example, that *DJ Penize*, 2007, a glossy black, bell-like shape that vaguely echoes the human body, with a ballpoint pen encased in resin stuck on its "head," is a portrait of a lonely office worker in a disco. But this, of course, is simply my own reading.

In their unruly lack of logic, Bauer's paintings, drawings and sculptures reiterate: you can't rehearse a painting or an emotional reaction, and you cannot always demand that either your materials or your imagination behave themselves. A painting is not, and never has been, an explanation—and

und dunkler Bereich links vom zentralen Bild an Barcodes im Supermarkt erinnert.

Bauers Malerei erscheint in Schatten und gemischten Lichtverhältnissen besser aufgehoben – ich stelle mir vor, dass sie in Zwielicht oder in der frühen Morgendämmerung aufblühen, oder dass sie an finsteren, verhangenen Nachmittagen zur Ruhe kommen, wenn der graue Himmel die Tiefe ihrer Farben verstärkt. Sepia schimmert mit all seinen Anklängen von Tod, Verfall und Erinnerung wie eine dünne Furnierschicht auf vielen dieser Bilder. Bei Pol 1 (Smart Estrus) *(2005) zum Beispiel ist ein abgetrennter Kopf aus fleischigen Wucherungen, Wülsten und einem einzelnen Glotzauge gebildet – ganz so als gäbe es nichts Schlimmeres, als die Unfähigkeit zu sehen. Leinwände sind mit bösen, ja sogar grotesken Figuren und unvermittelten Tonalitätsschwankungen übersät: Löcher (als wäre gar nichts wasserdicht), Flecken von düsterem Grün und eine seltsame zwischen Rosa und Grau changierende Haut treiben über einem leuchtenden, gemusterten Banner dahin. Eine saubere, schwarzweisse Feder entspriesst dem Kopf dieses Wesens. Bei allem Surrealismus, der hier im Spiel ist, handelt es sich doch aber auch um ein feierliches, sonderbar würdiges Porträt; wie die Hommage an einen lange verblichenen Aristokraten und für eine zukünftige Familie gemalt, spricht es sein Geheimnis aus, ohne sich dafür zu entschuldigen. In ähnlicher Weise erscheint einem* Pol 3 (Kamerad Säckle) *(2005) – das Bild des schwebenden Kopfes eines hirschartigen Tiers mit einem hell leuchtenden Augapfel, umgeben von etwas, das ich nur als eine Art milchiges Ektoplasma zu beschreiben weiss, das über einer einzelnen, pinkfarbenen Träne hängt – wie ein Zeitreisender; schwer zu sagen jedoch, ob der aus der Vergangenheit oder aus der Zukunft kommt.*

Während die Kohlezeichnungen flüssig, schnell und unkorrigiert sind – wie direkt vom Gehirn übertragene Kompositionen –, setzt Bauer die Ölfarbe ein, um mit einer Idee zu ringen, um sie zu färben und zu stauchen, wenn ihre Gestalt sich abzeichnet. Dies führt dazu, dass die Oberflächen dieser Gemälde eine starke Texturierung aufweisen – locker und traumverloren aufgelegte Farbschwaden treffen hart auf kreidige Pigmenttropfen oder harte grafische Linien. Bei näherer Betrachtung werden in den geröteten Pinks, den blutroten und ramponierten Beiges, die mit dem Pfirsichbraun ringen, und in den rauen Farbflächen, die sich über den mit giftigem Grün und haarfeinen dunklen Lineaturen versehenen weichen Grund ausbreiten, Spuren eines Kampfes ablesbar. Oft steigt unerwartet ein Gefühl von Leichtigkeit aus dem leimartigen Schlamm auf. Zum Beispiel materialisiert sich der locker angelegte Umriss einer Figur in einem neueren, in opulenten Schichten angelegten Bild, Bad Harvest *(2008), aus einem erdigen, aus dicken, geradezu skulpturalen Flächen aus schmutzigweisser Farbe, denen mit grosser Eleganz gestaltete Formen gegenüber stehen: zwei weiche, goldene Kugeln schwingen dort wie Christbaumkugeln, während auf der anderen Seite ein eleganter geometrischer Armausläufer sich mit einer an eine Tonscherbe erinnernden Form in Balance hält; ein Vögelchen mit einem violetten Kopf, das über einem Zebramuster und einer farbigen Linie von einem federähnlichen Schnabel herabhängt, lässt an Teppichknüpfereien von Stammeskulturen denken. Unerklärlicherweise verläuft*

it will always choose to hide as much as it reveals. Bauer's art is a space where the imaginary becomes physical. It's a space that cannot, on any level, be mistaken for a literal reflection of the world; however potent the image, its descriptions are illusory, its relationship to history, at best suggestive. It's a world that is complicated and inconclusive—qualities that here are strangely comforting: sometimes absurdity can feel like a kind of celebration. As a culture, we are so glutted on images designed to be understood in the blink of an eye, that an art that resists swift readings—that demands you slow down, and look and respond without a predetermined conclusion, and that encourages your imagination to rise above the mire—can engender a rare, if unsettling, pleasure.

Jennifer Higgie is co-editor of *Frieze*.

eine saubere, dunkelgrüne Linie diagonal von oben rechts nach unten links über das ganze Bild. Zwar hat schon der Titel des Bildes etwas Unheilvolles, doch schaffen seine Komposition und die eingesetzte fieberhafte Einbildungskraft hier eine gespenstisch-mythologische Atmosphäre – als warte nur ein Stückchen jenseits der Grenzen unseres Fassungsvermögens etwas Überwältigendes, möglicherweise auch Unheimliches.

Bauers monochrome und abstrakte Skulpturen weisen gegenüber der Malerei eine ganz andere Gestimmtheit auf, sie stehen wie anthropomorphe Wächter auf einfachen, ja sogar schwächlich wirkenden Trägern vor den Gemälden. Sie sind oft wider Erwarten ausladend, üppig, wirken ein bisschen undurchsichtig und charaktervoll. Obwohl sie in ihren formalen Eigenschaften unbestimmt sind, kommt man nicht umhin, ihre ausgreifenden Umrisse als geniale Phalli oder als Nasen zu deuten, die aus klumpigen, beseelt wirkenden Köpfen hervortreten (ich kann nicht sagen, warum sie mir ein wenig traurig, ja sogar herzzereissend erscheinen). Sie schmelzen, hängen herab, versuchen stramm zu stehen oder geradeaus zu starren, ihre Oberflächen bestehen aus harten, oftmals auch glänzenden Materialien – aus Glasfliesen oder glänzend schwarz, leuchtend weiss, tiefviolett oder limettengrün gefasstem Stuckgips. Als handle es sich um materialisierte Gedanken, sind den Skulpturen hin und wieder gewöhnliche Alltagsgegenstände beigegeben: Reiskuchen, Nikotinpflaster, ein Schreibstift oder in Harz gegossene Pillen. Hier haben wir es mit Skulpturen zu tun, die sich für jede Art der Vorspiegelung eignen. Ich könnte zum Beispiel schwören, dass DJ Penize (2007) – eine glänzend schwarze, glockenartige Form, die vage an eine menschliche Körperform erinnert und aus deren „Kopf" ein in Giessharz eingeschlossener Kugelschreiber steckt – eigentlich das Porträt eines vereinsamten Büroangestellten in einer Disco ist. Aber das ist natürlich nur meine persönliche Deutung.

Mit ihrem unbändigen Mangel an Logik sagen uns Bauers Gemälde, Zeichnungen und Skulpturen immer wieder aufs Neue: ein Bild oder eine emotionale Reaktion kann man nicht proben, und man kann auch nicht erwarten, dass sich einem die Materialien oder die Einbildungskraft stets zu Willen sind. Ein Gemälde ist nie und war nie eine Erklärung – und es wird immer ebenso viel verbergen wollen wie es enthüllt. Bauers Kunst bildet einen Raum, in dem das Imaginäre zu etwas Physischem wird. Ein Raum, den man auf keiner Ebene als buchstäbliche Widerspiegelung der Welt missverstehen kann – so wirkungsmächtig das Bild auch sein mag, seine Beschreibungen sind illusorisch, sein Verhältnis zur Geschichte erschöpft sich bestenfalls in Andeutungen. Es ist eine komplizierte und zu keiner verbindlichen Aussage fähige Welt – wobei diese Eigenschaften hier seltsamerweise beruhigend wirken: die Absurdität erscheint einem manchmal wie ein Fest. Unsere Kultur überfüttert uns dermassen mit Bildern, die in Sekundenbruchteilen verstehbar sein sollen, dass eine Kunst, die sich flinker Auslegung entzieht – die einem Verlangsamung, genaues Hinsehen und vorurteilsloses Reagieren abverlangt und einen ermutigt, seine Einbildungskraft aus dem gewohnten Sumpf aufsteigen zu lassen –, zu einem seltenen, wenn auch beunruhigenden Genuss führen kann.

Jennifer Higgie ist Mitherausgeberin von Frieze.

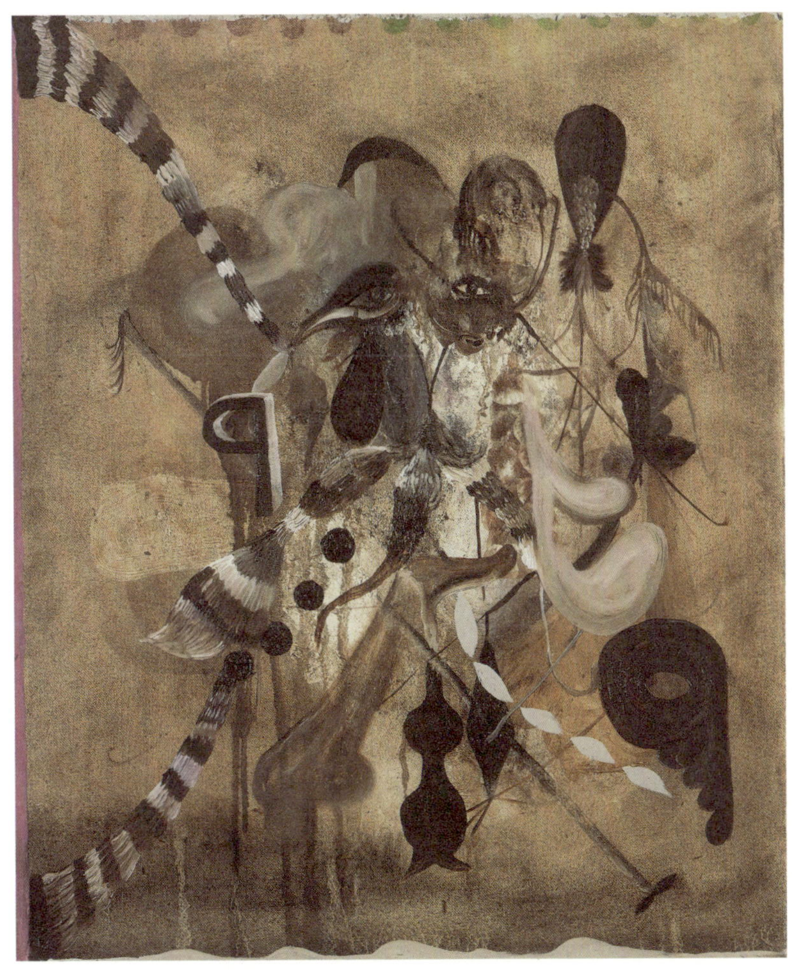

Prizcilla, 2006, oil on canvas, 60 x 50 cm

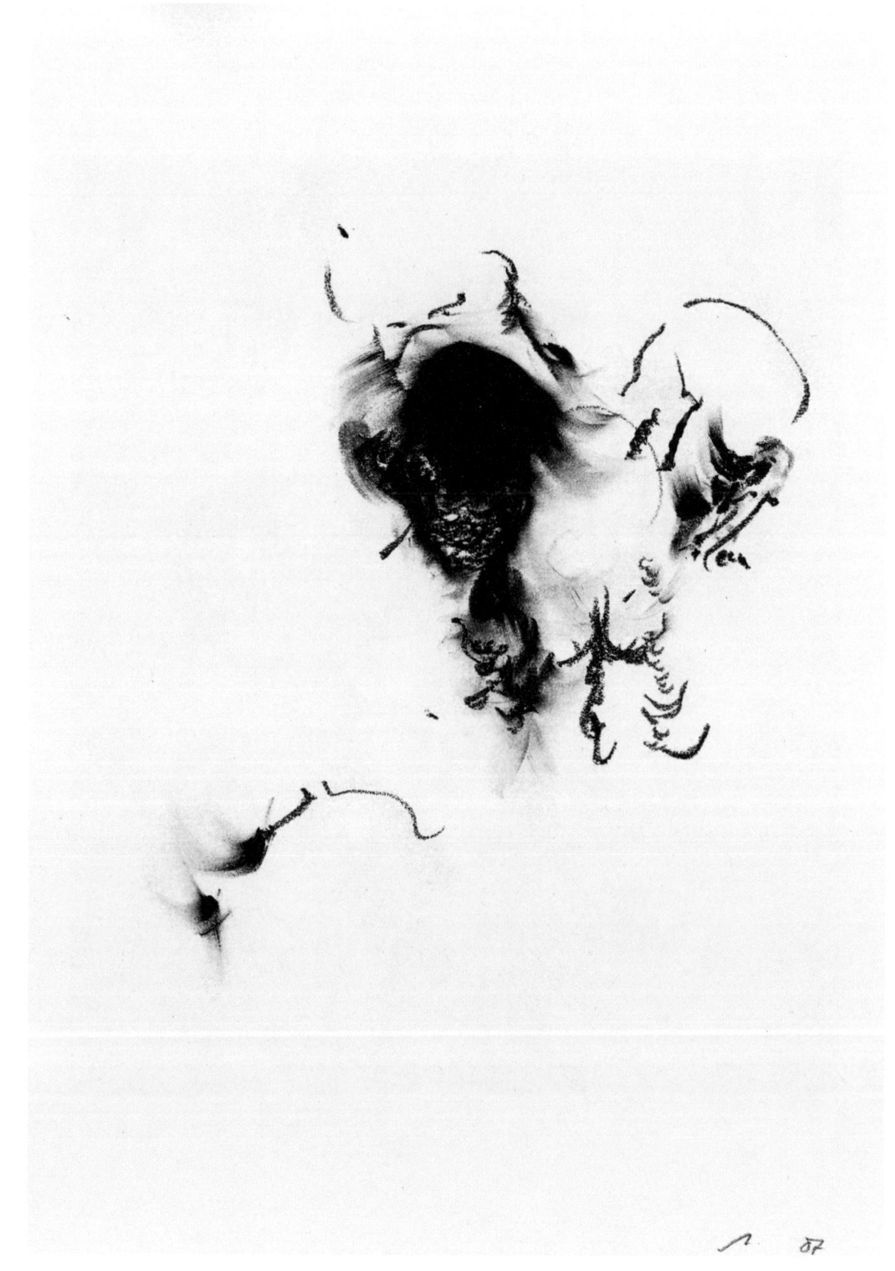

Shake Your Libido, 2007, charcoal on paper, 42 x 29.7 cm

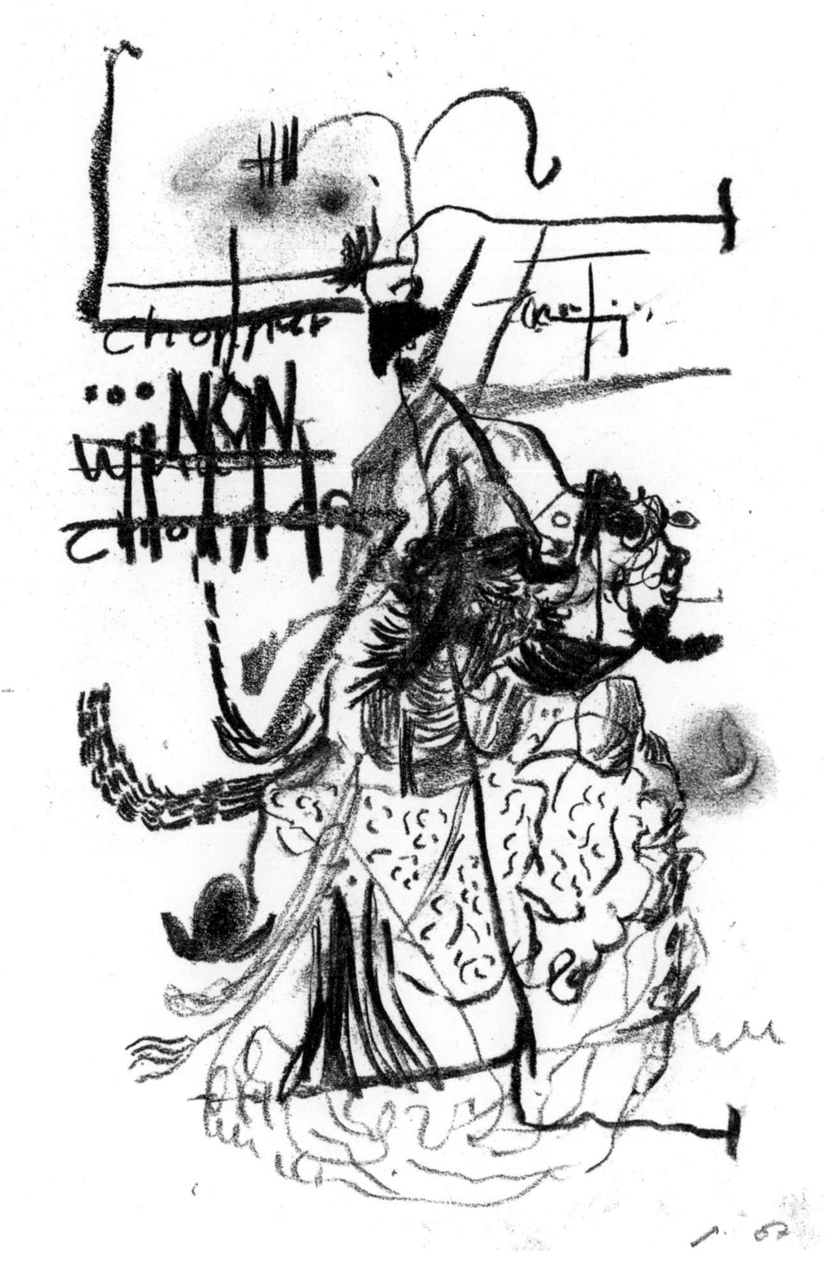

Wolfberg, 2007, charcoal on paper, 29.7 x 21 cm

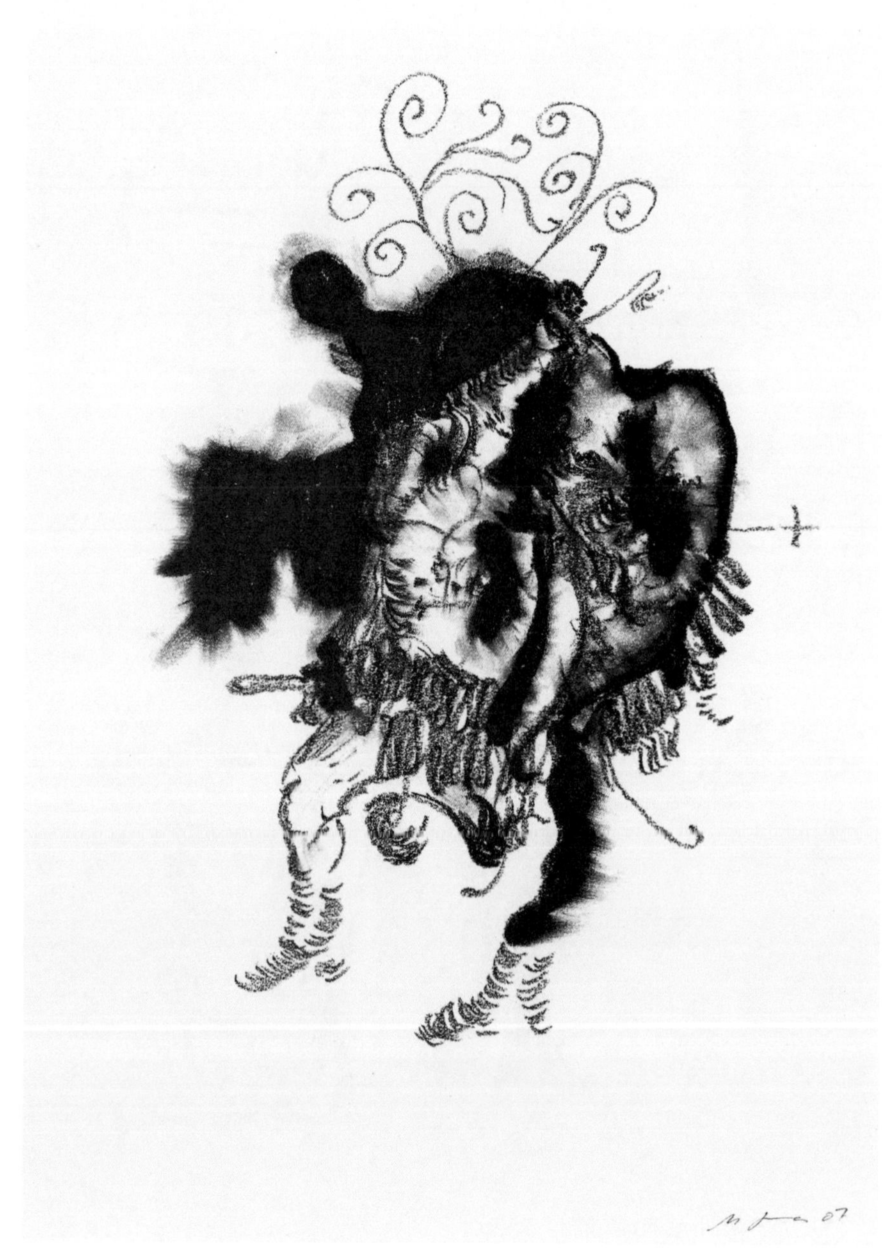

Einer von Norden, 2007, charcoal on paper, 42 x 29.7 cm

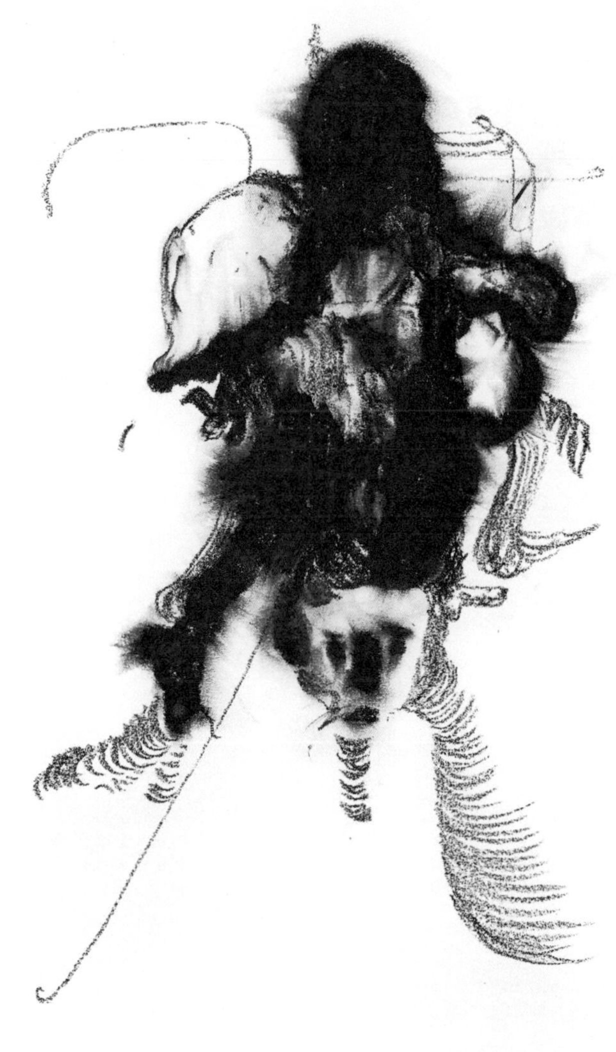

Einer von Westen, 2007, charcoal on paper, 42 x 29.7 cm

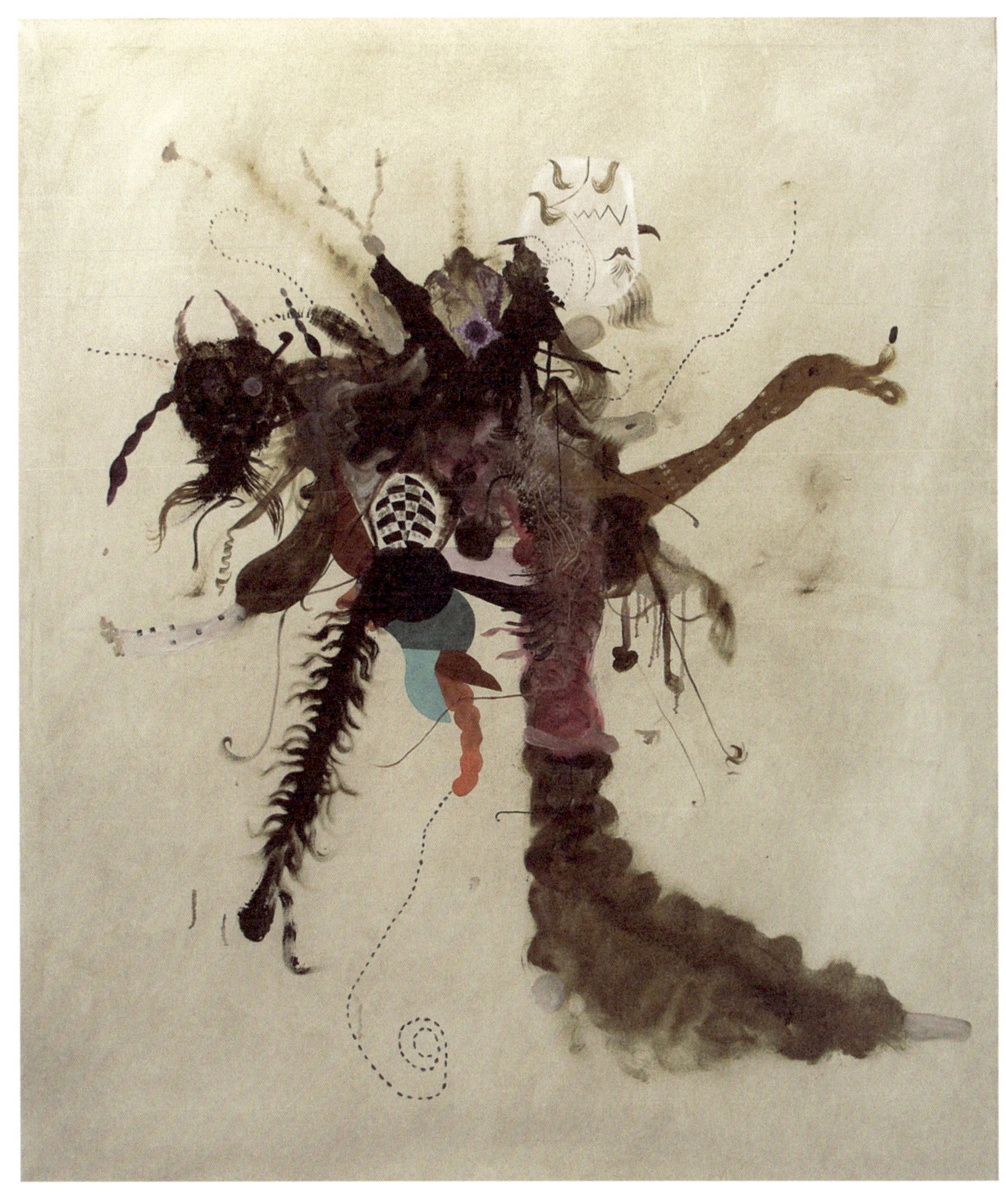

Indianapolis, 2006, oil on canvas, 150 x 130 cm

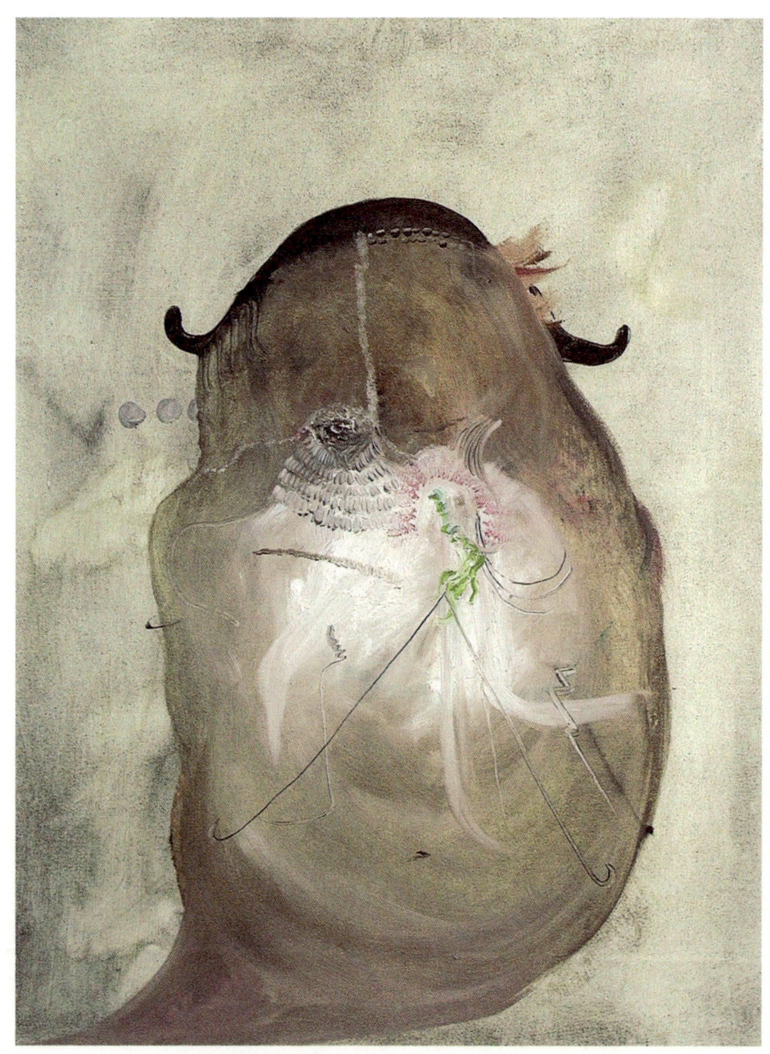

Sandi, 2004, oil on canvas, 80 x 60 cm

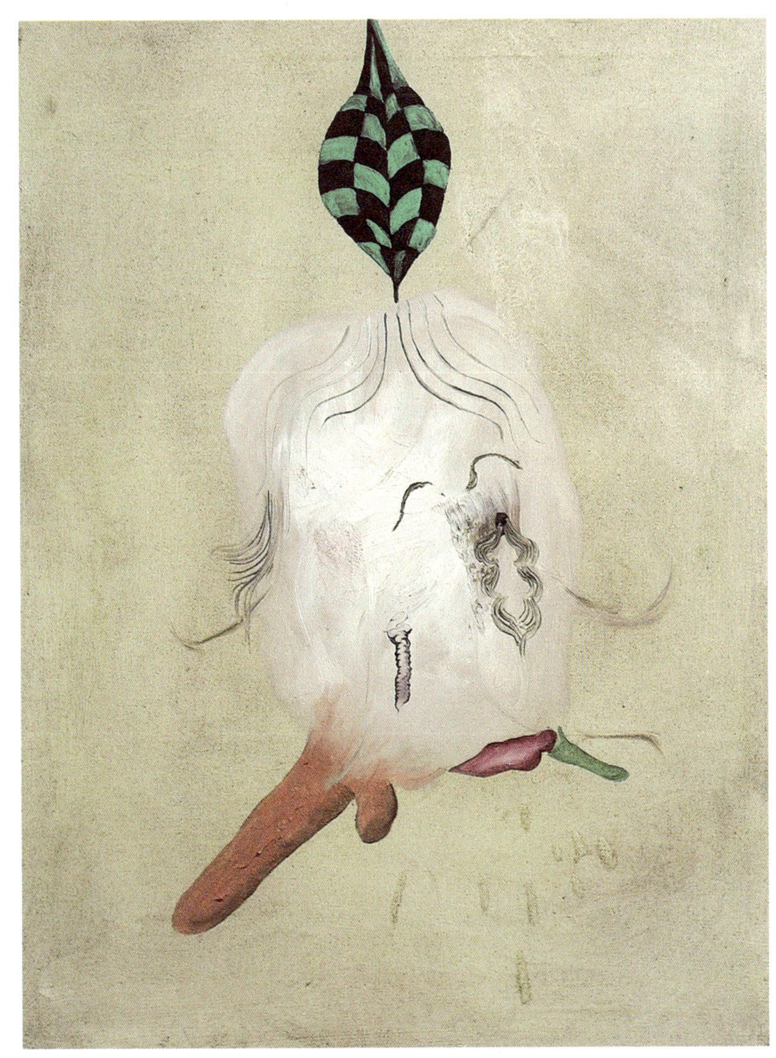

Mandi, 2004, oil on canvas, 80 x 60 cm

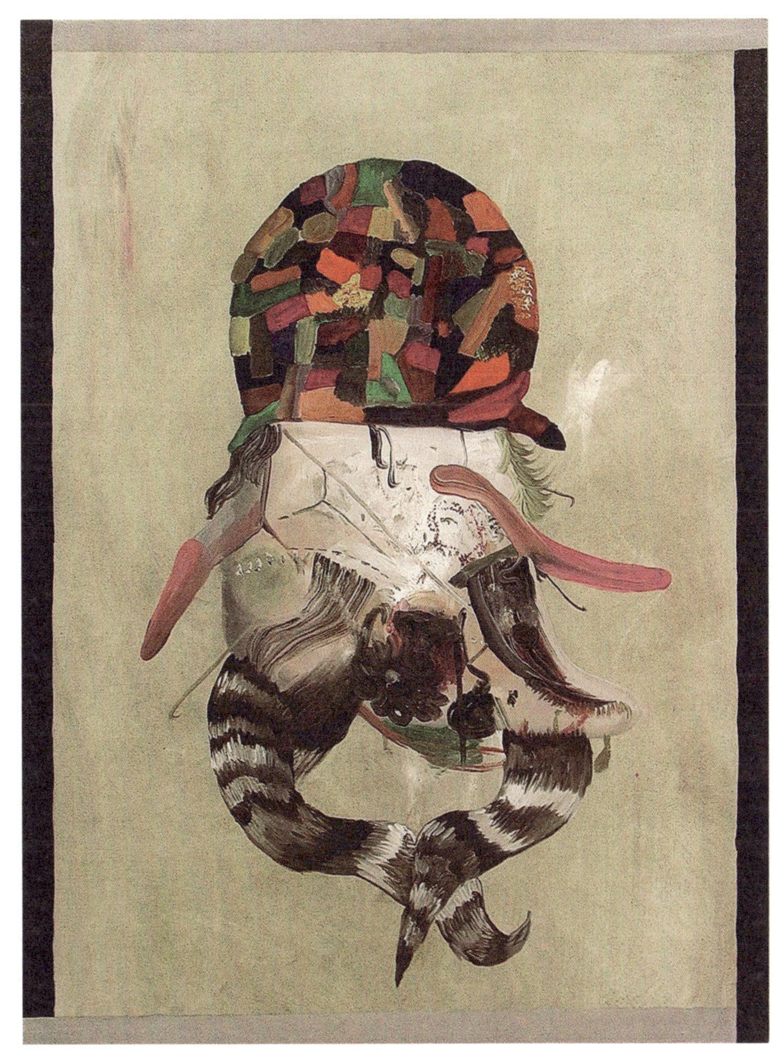

Graf Bernadotte Indien, 2004, oil on canvas, 80 x 60 cm

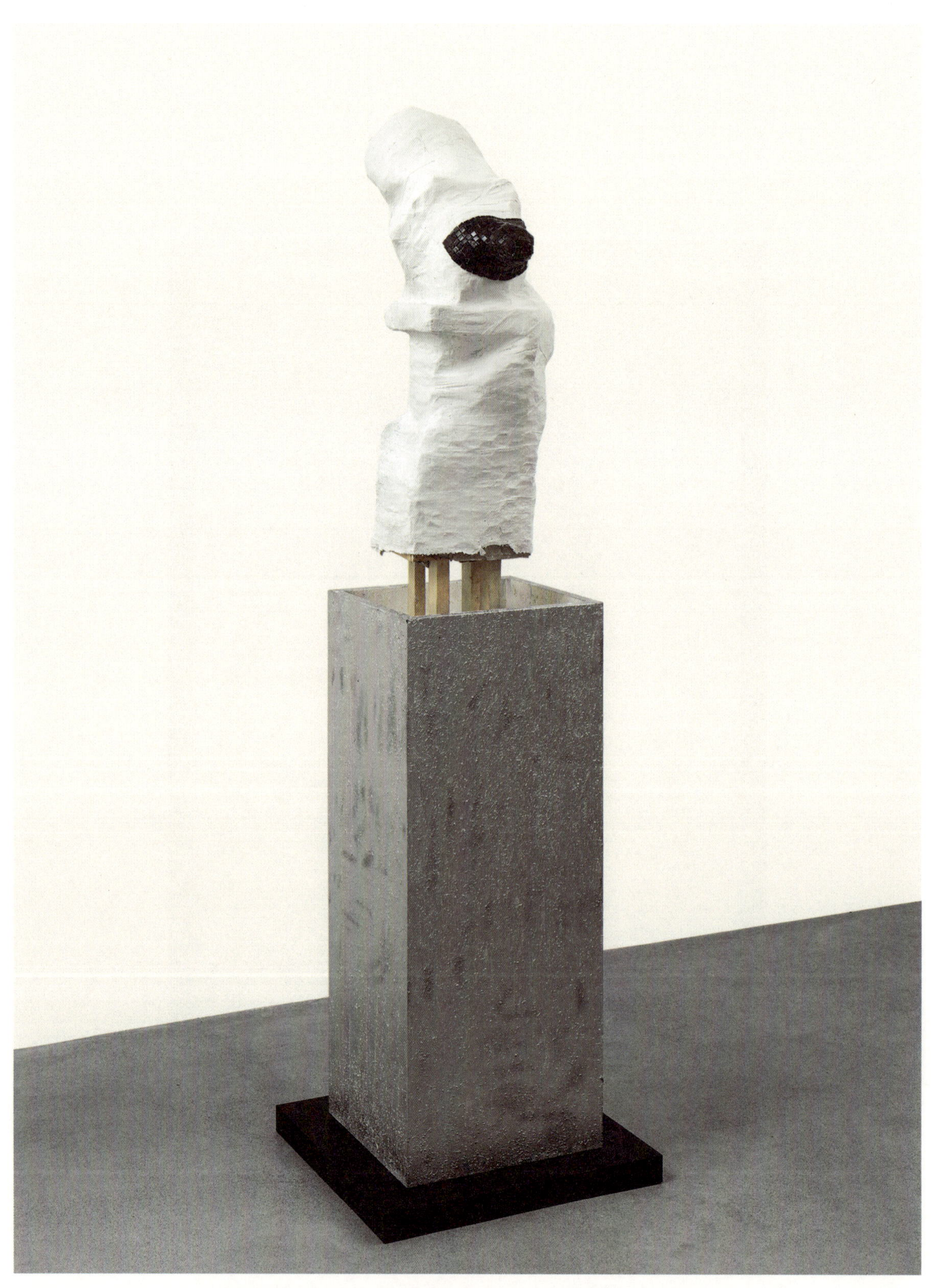

DJ Muppins Infinity, 2007, glass, plaster, wood, 197 x 61 x 55 cm

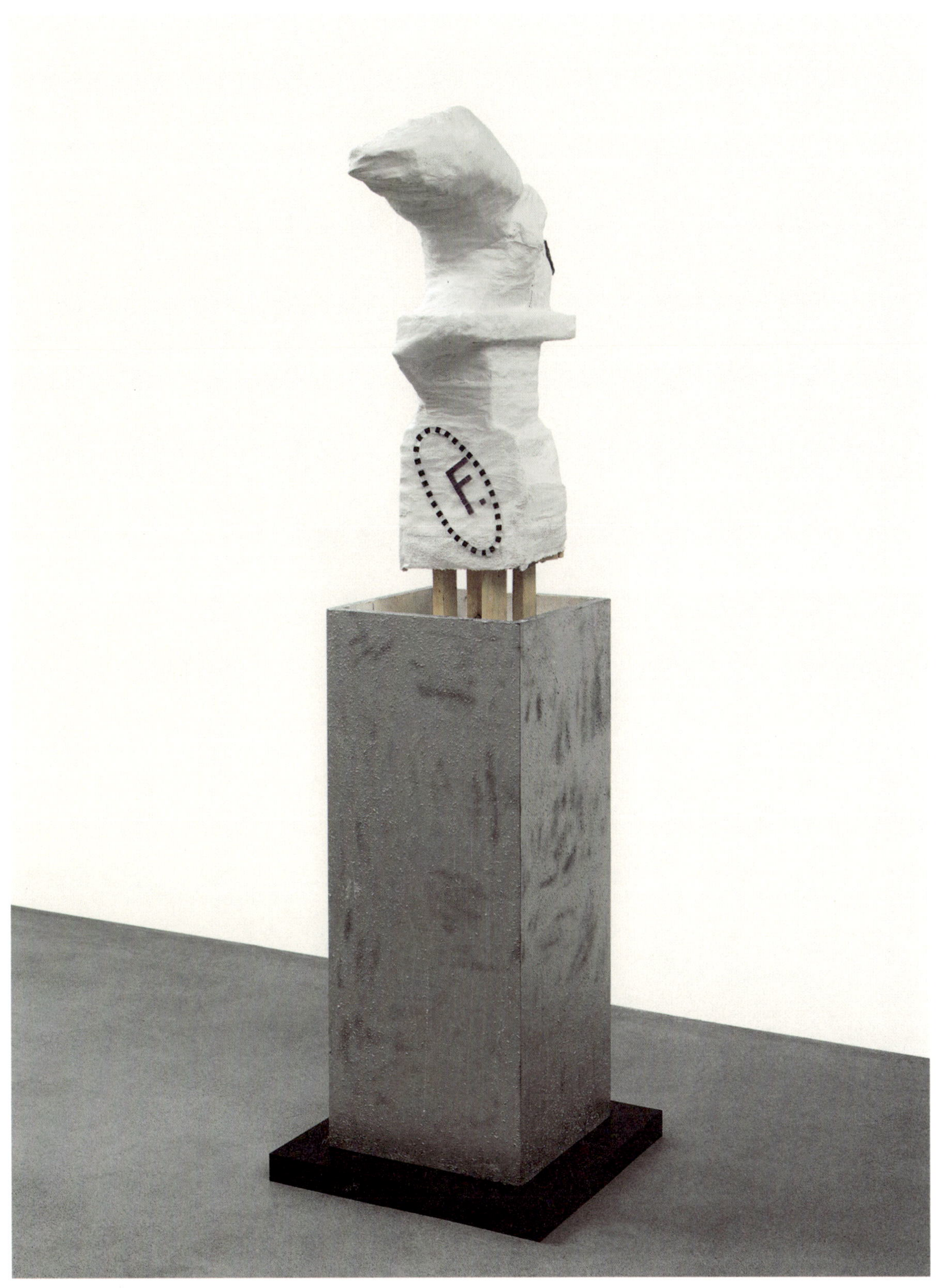

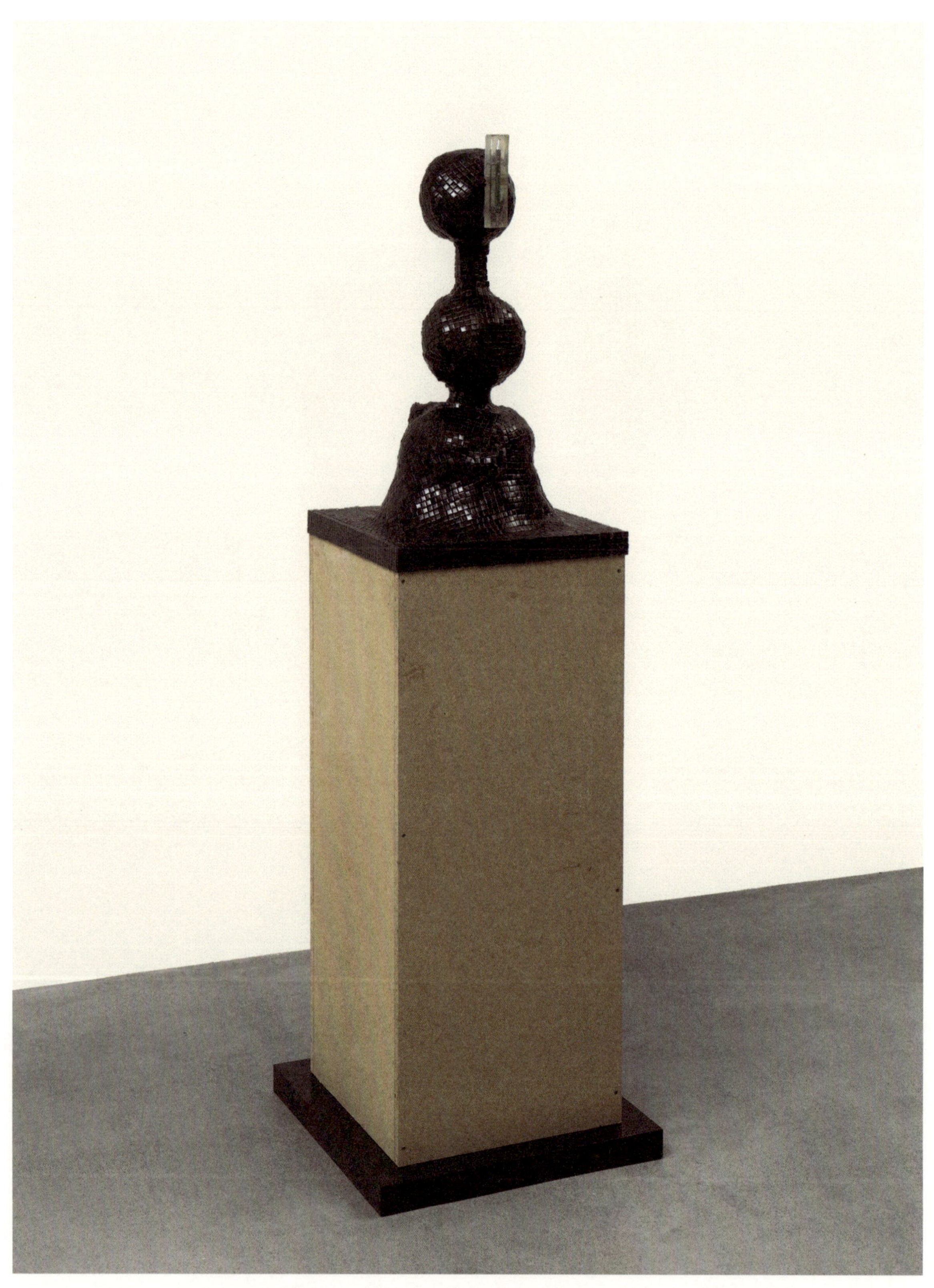

DJ Penize, 2007, glass, resin, ballpoint pen, plaster, wood, 175 x 55 x 55 cm

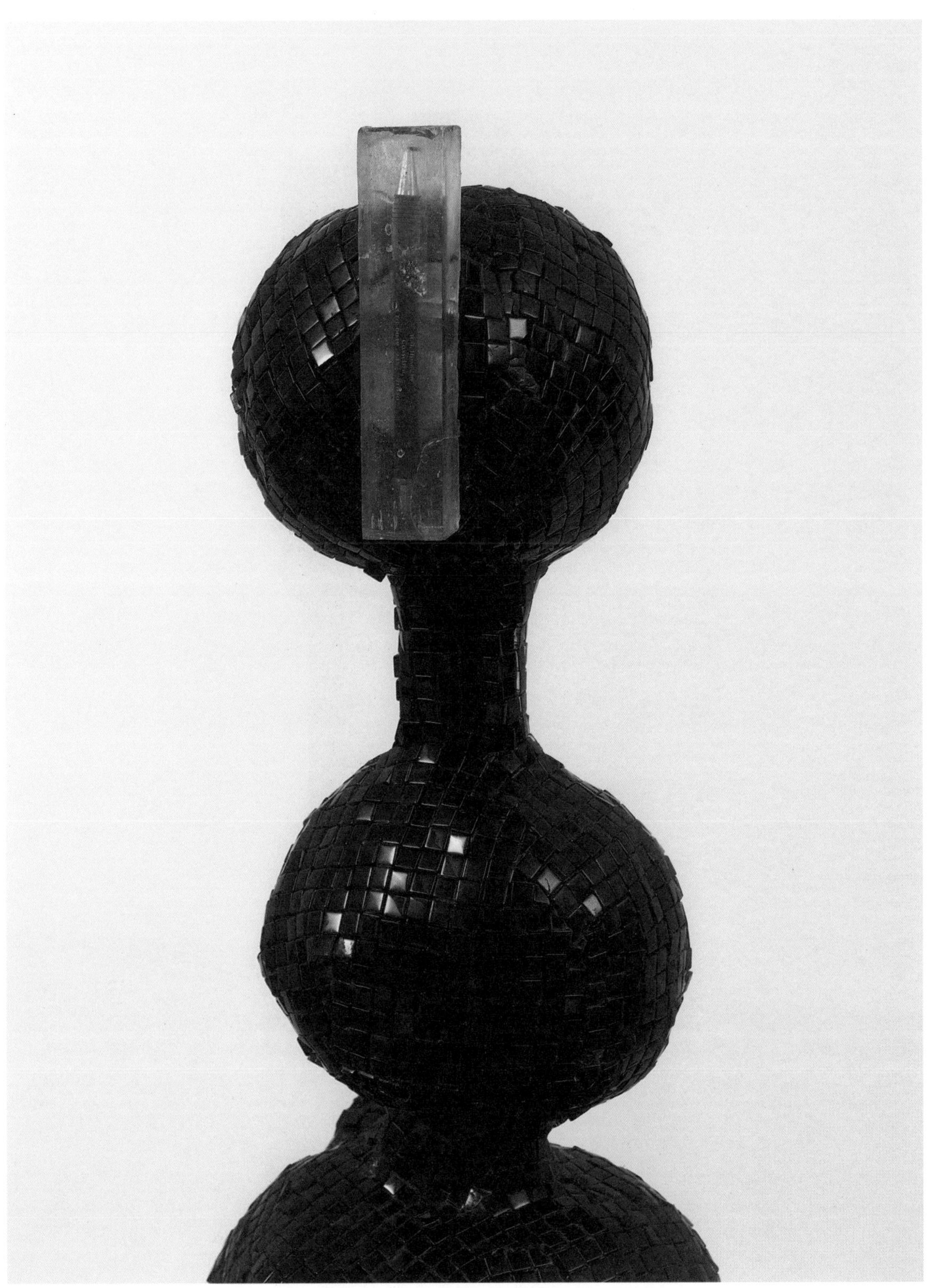

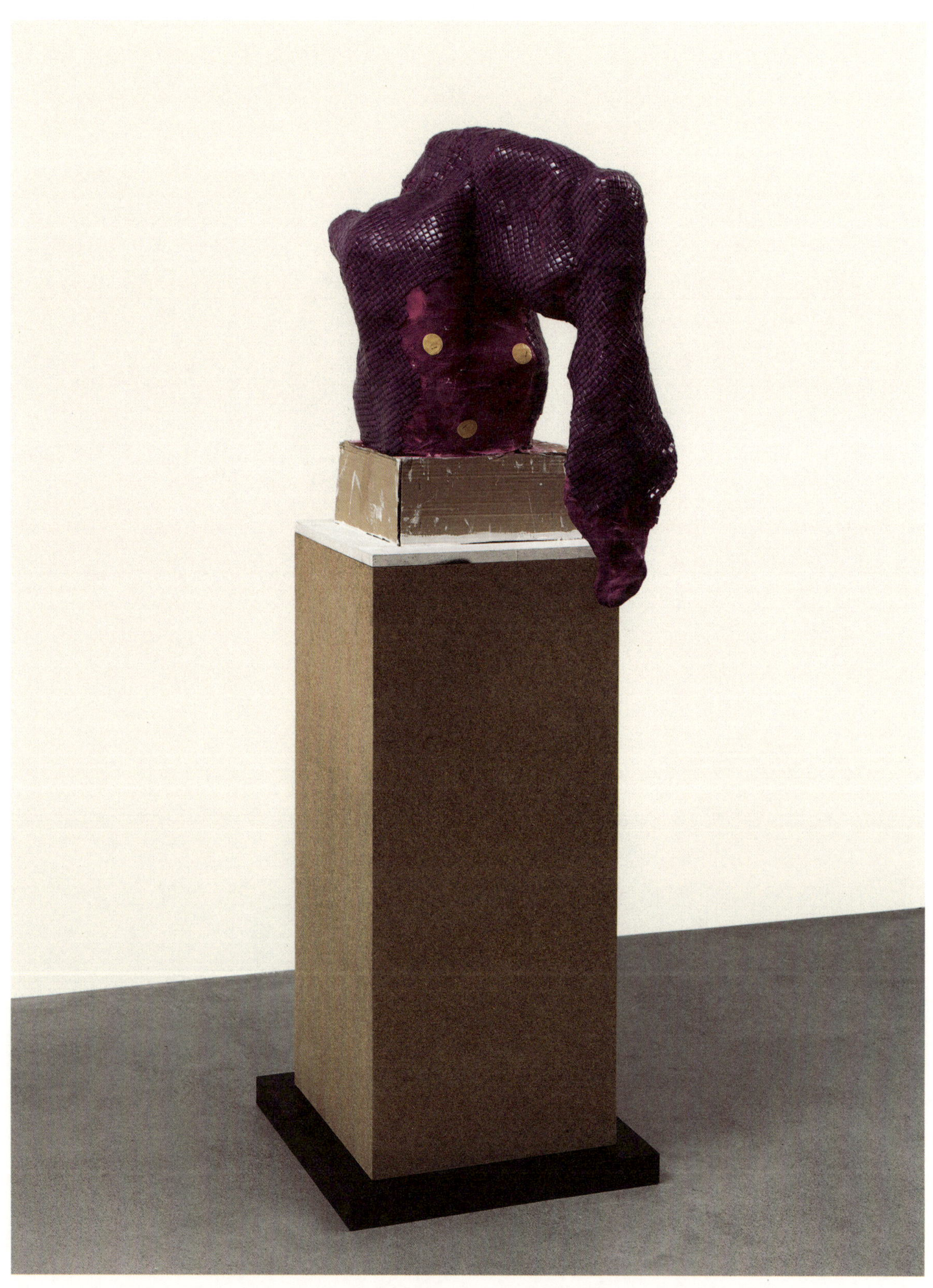

DJ Pennydenny B, 2007, glass, painted plaster, cardboard, nicotine patch, wood, 175 x 55 x 71 cm

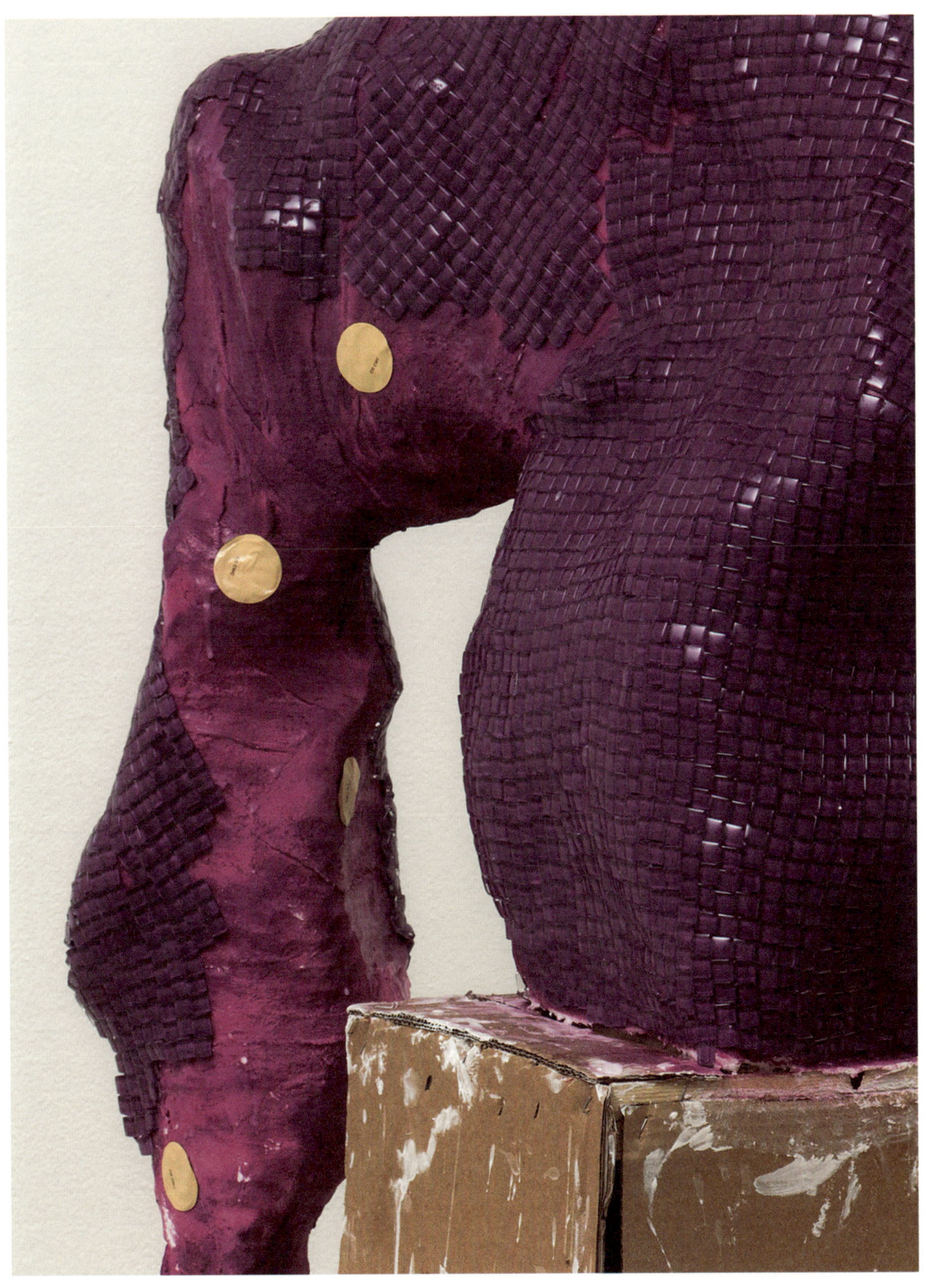

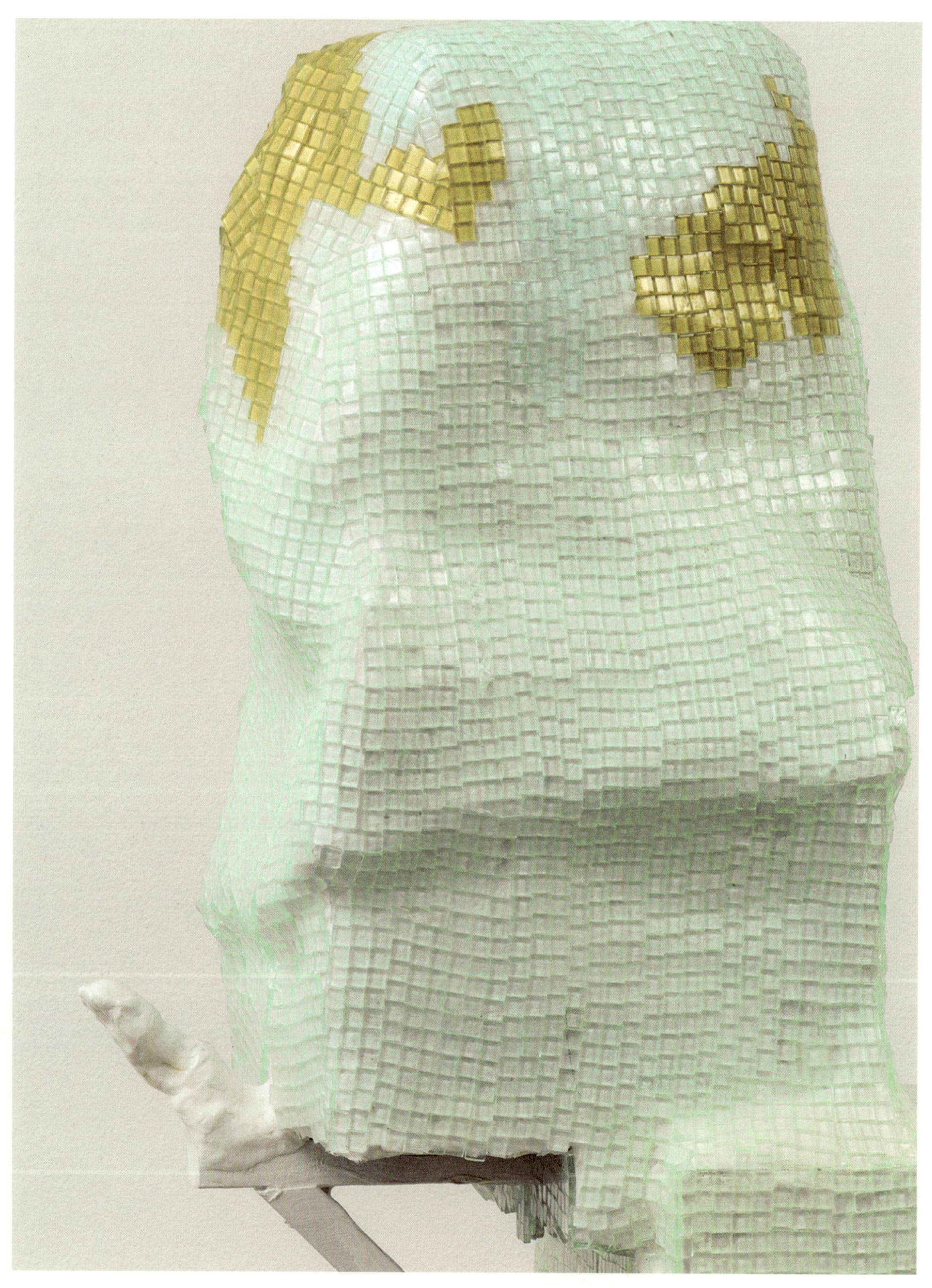
DJ Ponyhotello, 2007, glass, plaster, wood, 187 x 76.5 x 55 cm

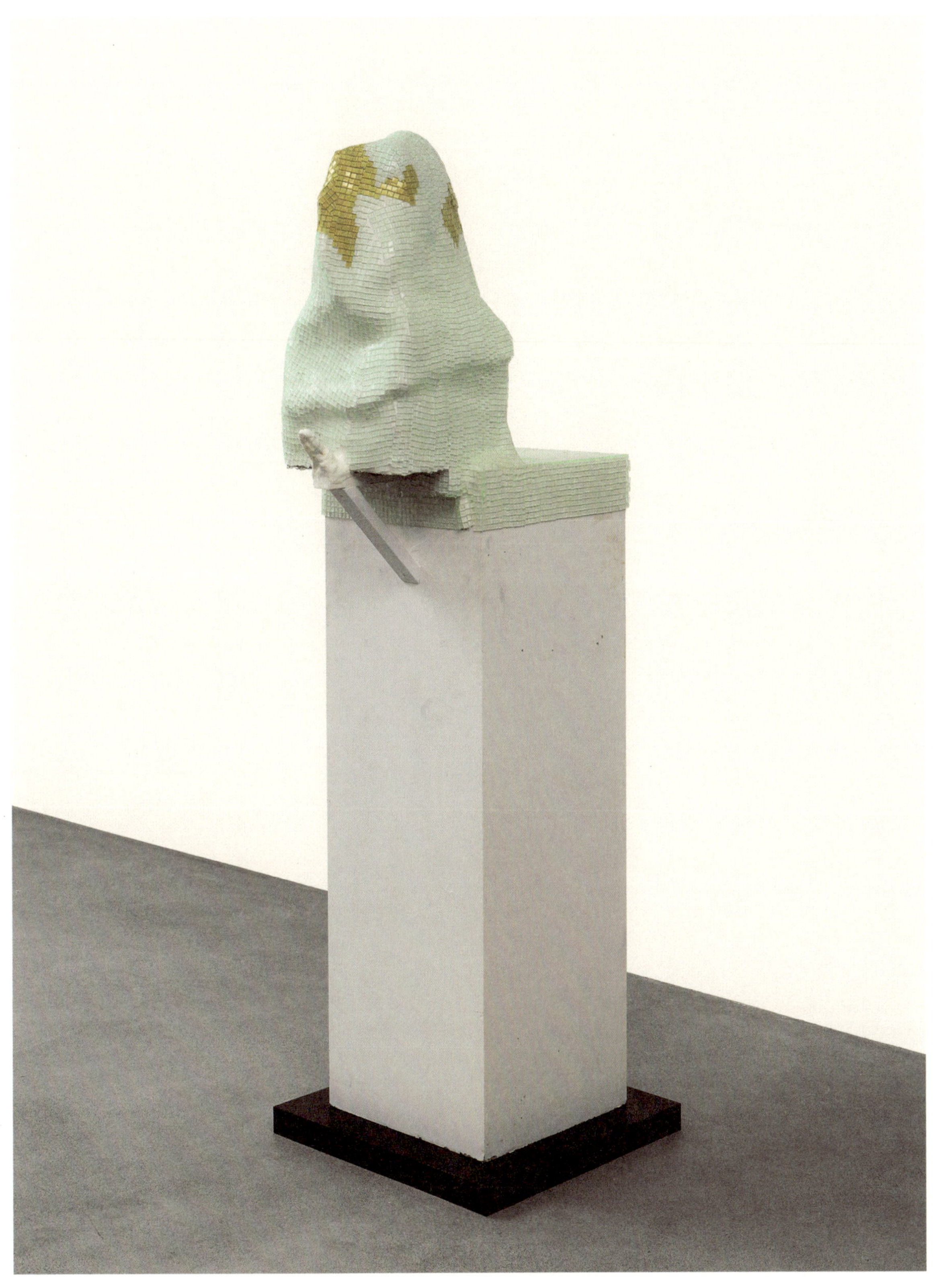

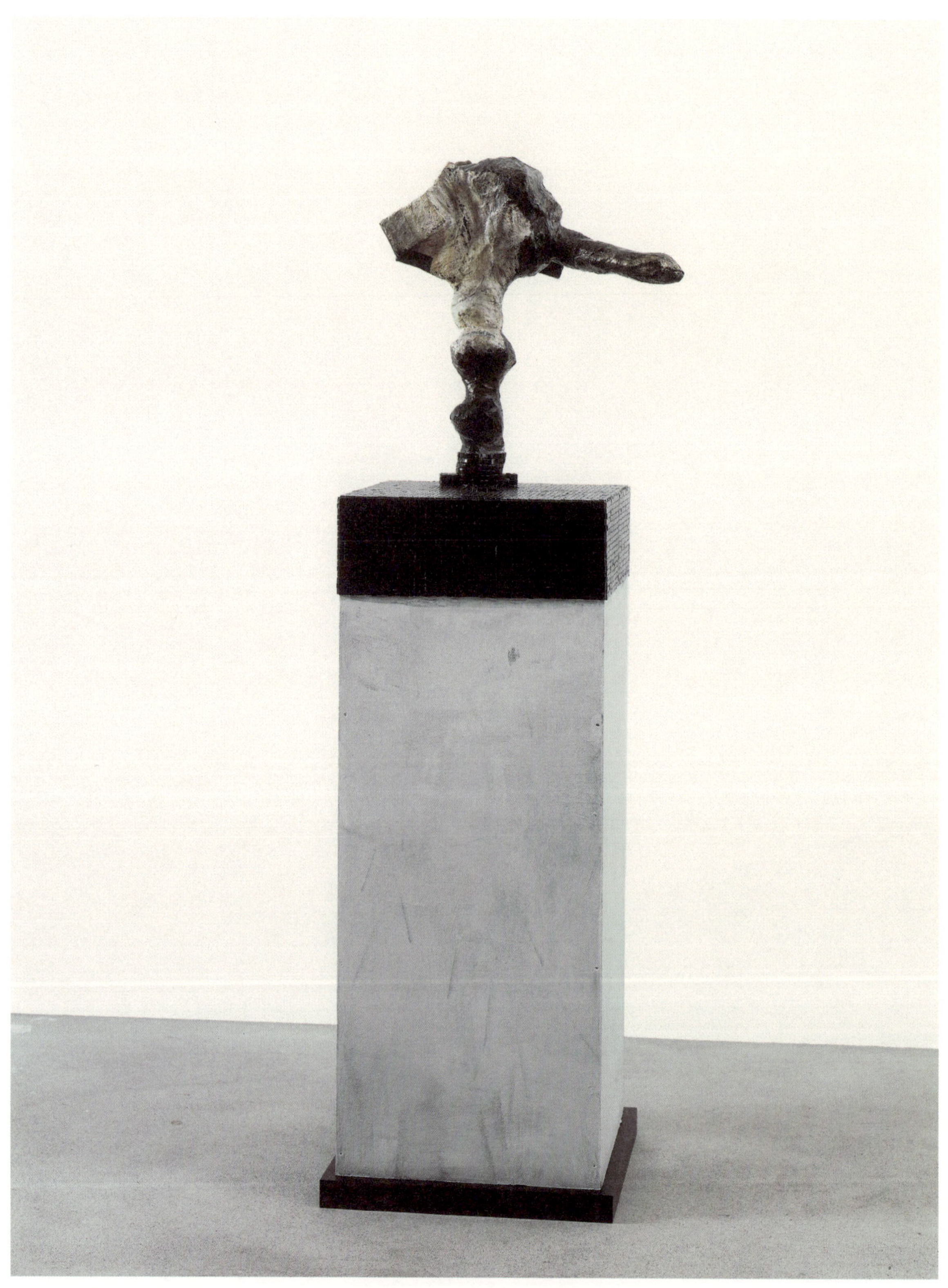

Burzum, 2008, glass, plaster, wood, 160 x 50 x 50 cm

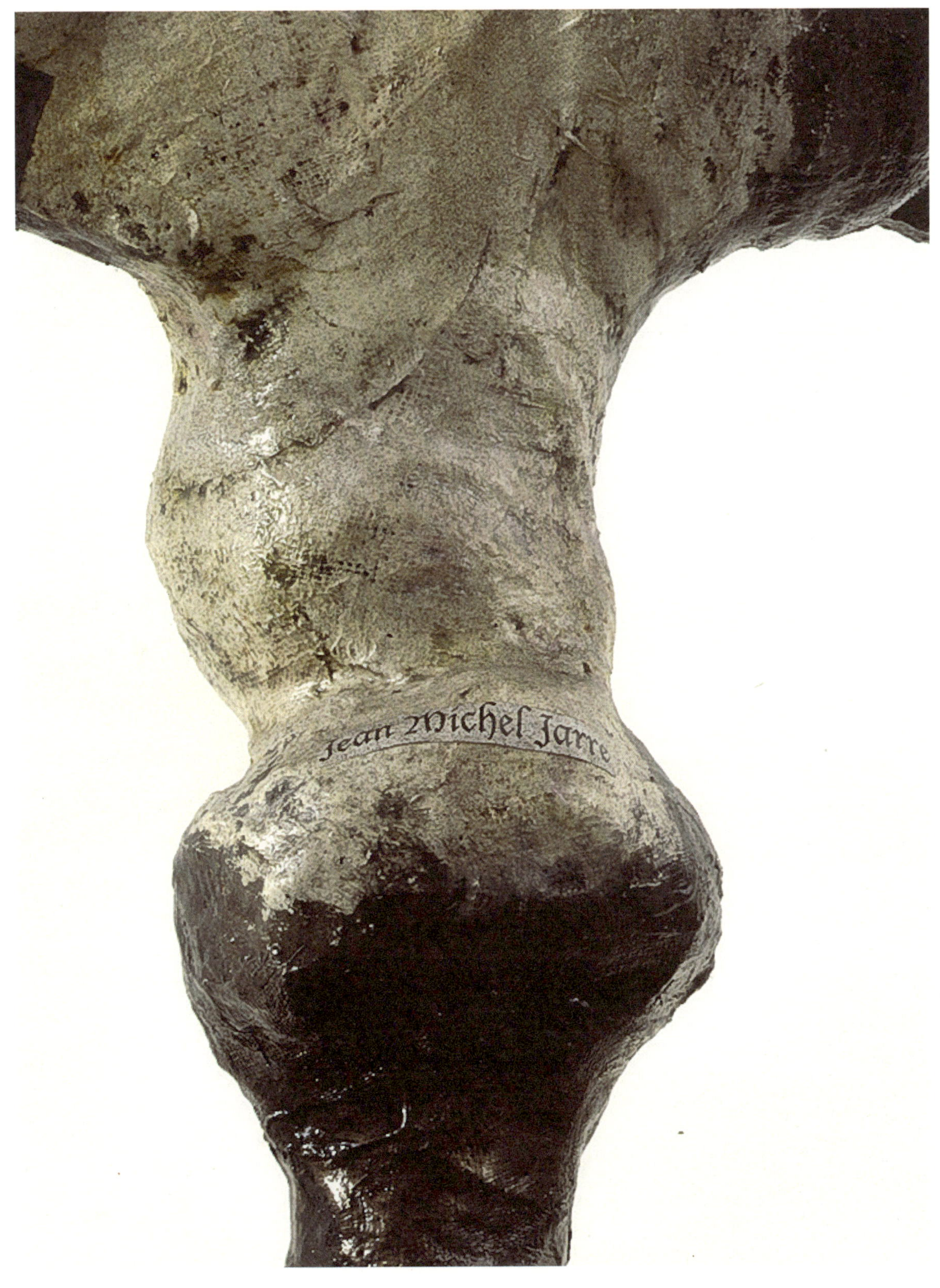

Jean Michel Jarre

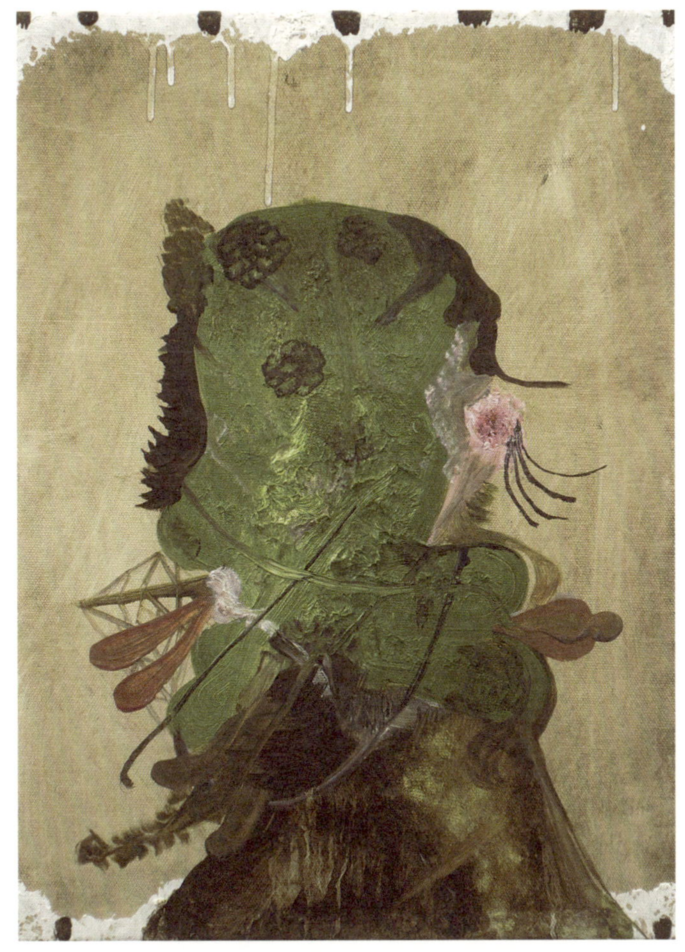

Harry Booth, 2006, oil on canvas, 40 x 30 cm

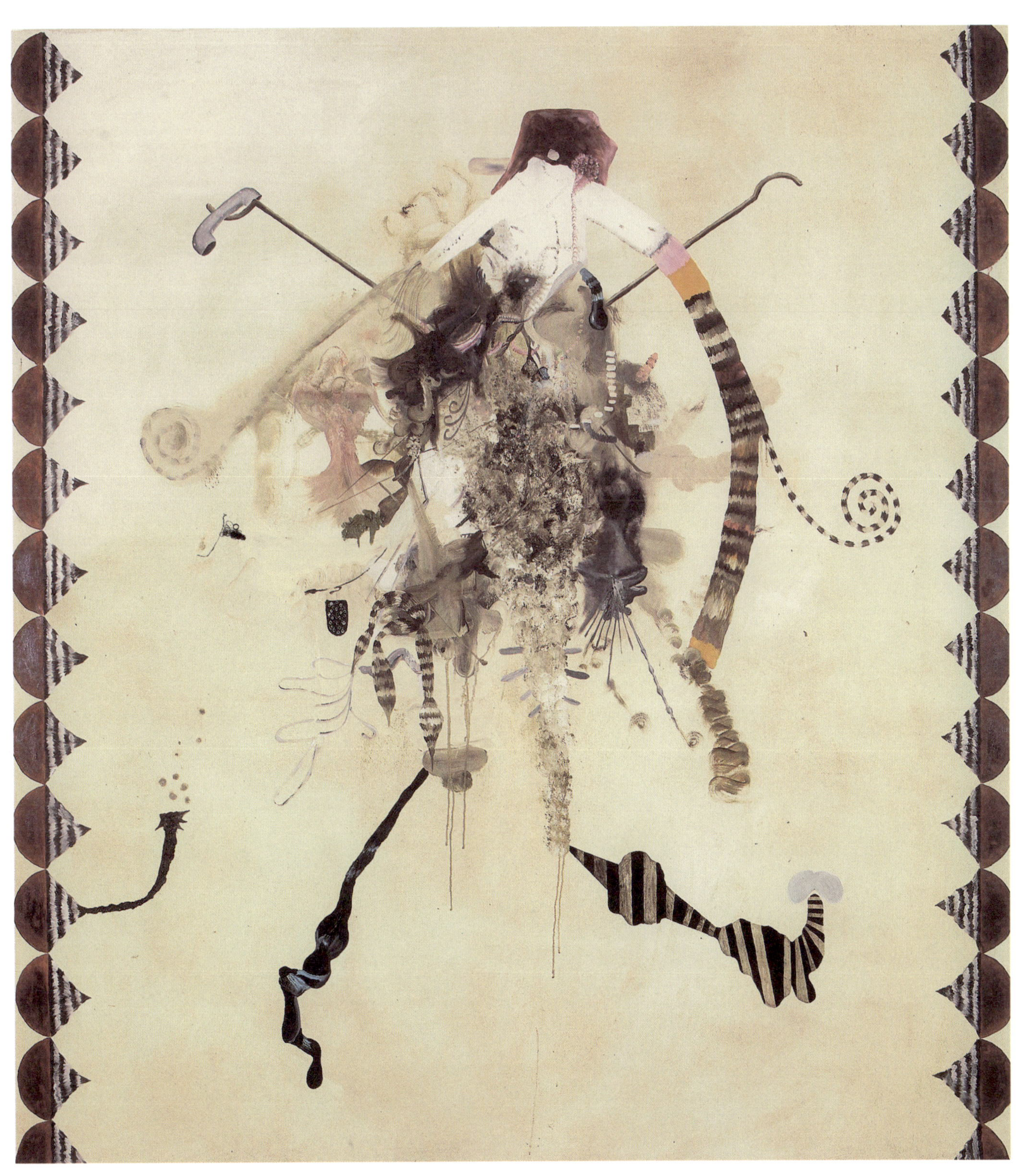

Nobsi Mob, 2006, oil on canvas, 210 x 190 cm

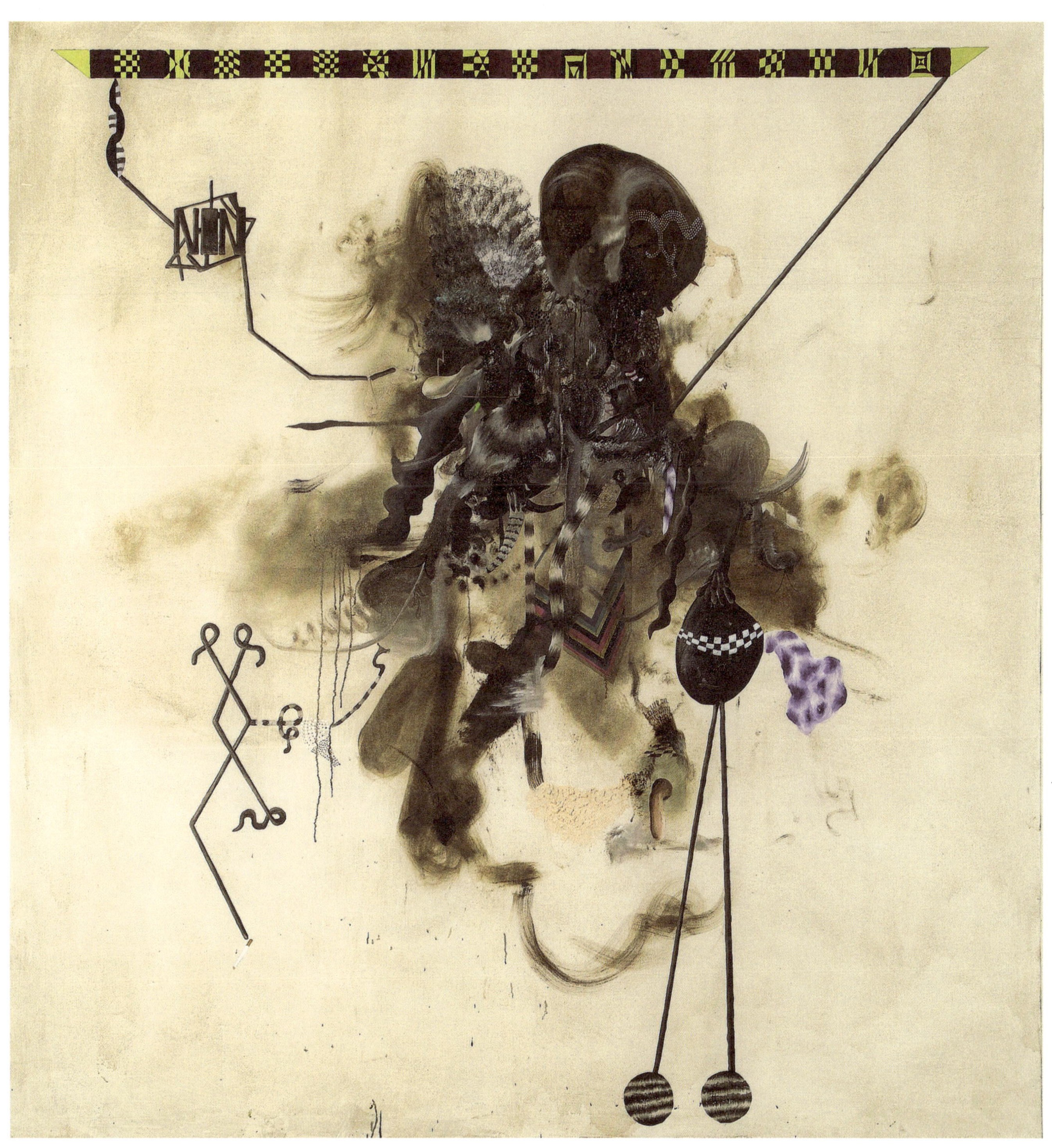

Blair Petrie–20 Million Years, 2007, oil on canvas, 200 x 190 cm

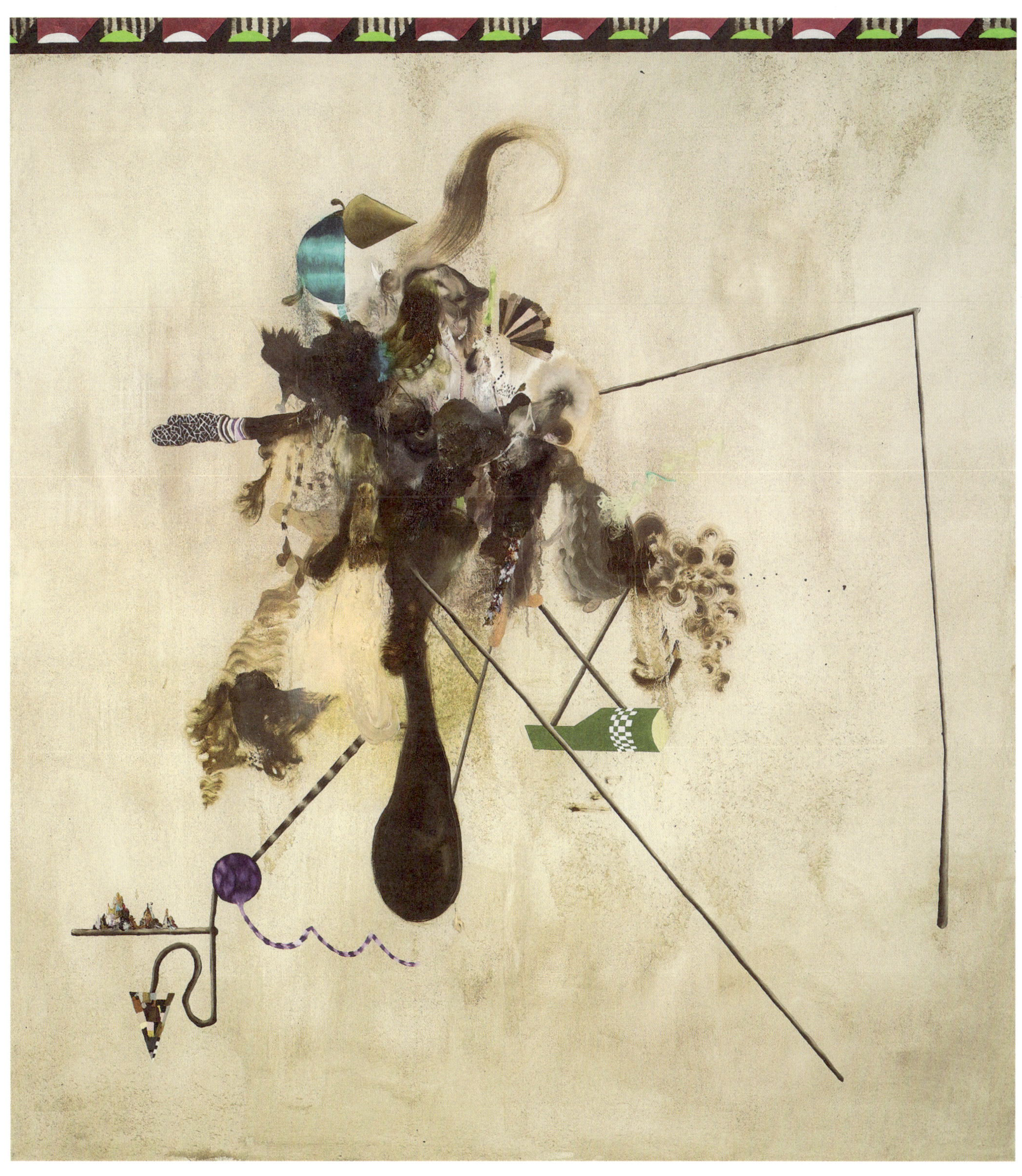

Basho Mob, 2007, oil on canvas, 290 x 190 cm

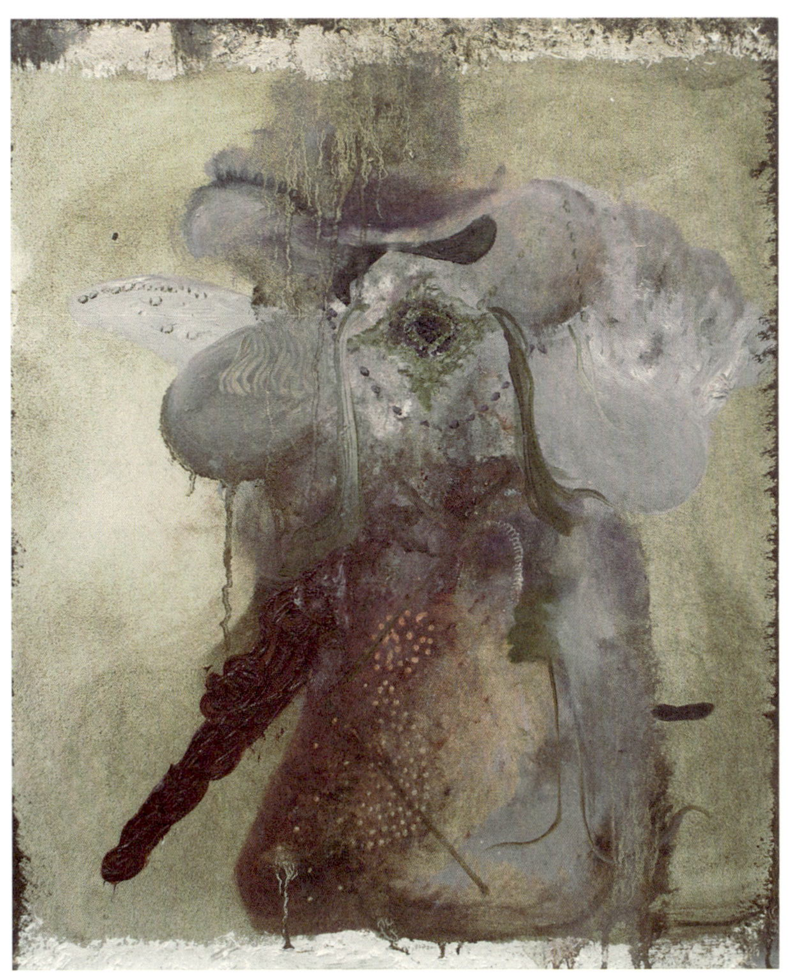

Bessy, 2006, oil on canvas, 60 x 50 cm

The Figure is Legion / *Die Figur ist Legion*
Stefanie Popp and Michael Bauer

Stefanie Popp: Do you know the tanuki statues that are often placed in or outside Japanese restaurants? They show the tanuki—the Japanese raccoon dog—as a fat-bellied comic figure with a leaf or a straw hat on its head, an empty sake bottle in one hand, and an IOU in the other (a debt that's never paid, because the tanuki is a highly frivolous, thoroughly mischievous creature, like a clumsy, bizarre brother of the clever fox). Moreover, and this is where it gets interesting, the tanuki has huge testicles that hang down to the ground. In earlier representations they are even used as drums or thrown over the animal's shoulders like a rucksack. As well as being extremely cute (as silly and jolly as it is gullible and absent-minded), the tanuki can expand its scrotum to huge dimensions and put it to a wide range of uses—as a blanket or cushion on which it curls up for a nap, or as an umbrella, a boat, a room, whatever happens to be needed.

Michael Bauer: That's a wonderful image. There are also pictures of a tanuki using its balls as a parachute. I like that. In my paintings, testicles—or sex organs in general—are never functional in a sexual sense. They're more like objects that have somehow been attached.

SP: Although the genitals in your paintings are identifiable as such, they don't correspond directly. They have a soft, amorphous quality, appearing rather formless and mutable. All in all, these lumpy, fleshy objects could be something like a versatile, unfixed counter-model to the phallic symbol. Or better still: a comment on and complement to it. Nicely playful and bizarre, versatile and mutable, like tanuki testicles.

MB: Yes. I think the phalli, especially in the Pol series, are rather sad appendages, robbed of their actual function. Like a last, sad gesture of potency. In that respect, they are a kind of reluctant counter-model. There's nothing scary about them, more easy-going, like your tanuki, as there's no longer a threat of penetration. It's more akin to waving. As if to briefly draw attention to something, a reminder it once existed. Only then to flop back down on the bed. The image of a tanuki sleeping on its own outspread scrotum really appeals to me.

Stefanie Popp: Kennst Du diese Tanuki-Statuen in bzw. vor japanischen Restaurants? Sie zeigen den Tanuki (Marderhund) als dickbäuchige Comicfigur, mit einem Blatt oder Strohhütchen auf dem Kopf, einer leeren Flasche Sake in der einen und einem Schuldschein in der anderen Hand (eine Rechnung die nie bezahlt wird, denn der Tanuki ist ein höchst unseriöses, und durch und durch verschmitztes Wesen; so eine Art plumper, skurriler Bruder des cleveren Fuchses) und, jetzt wird's interessant: grossen bis zum Boden baumelnden Hoden. In älteren Darstellungen werden die auch schon mal als Trommeln benutzt oder wie Rucksäcke über die Schultern geworfen.

Der Tanuki ist nämlich nicht nur unheimlich putzig, (so albern und mopsfidel wie leichtgläubig und geistesabwesend), vor allem kann er seinen Hodensack zu enormer Grösse expandieren und sehr vielfältig einsetzen z.B. als Decke oder Kissen auf dem er sich gemütlich zum Nickerchen zusammenrollt oder auch als Regenschutz, Boot oder Zimmer, was eben gerade so ansteht.

Michael Bauer: Das ist ein wunderbares Bild. Es gibt ja auch Abbildungen eines Tanuki, das seine Eier als Fallschirm benutzt. Das gefällt mir, die Hoden oder überhaupt die Sexualorgane in meinen Bildern haben ja auch nie eine Funktion im sexuellen Sinn. Die funktionieren ja auch eher als irgendwie angekoppelte Gegenstände.

SP: Diese Geschlechtsteile in deinen Bildern sind zwar als solche identifizierbar aber nicht direkt zuzuordnen. Die haben eine weiche, morphische Qualität, wirken eigentlich eher formfrei, verwandelbar.

In ihrer Gesamtheit könnten diese fleischig-klumpigen Gebilde so etwas wie ein vielfältiges, unfixiertes Gegenmodell zum Phallussymbol sein. Oder besser: Kommentar und Ergänzung dazu. Schön verspielt und bizarr, vielfältig und verwandelbar..., wie die Tanuki-Hoden.

MB: Ja. Ich glaube die Phalli, vor allem in den *Pol*-Bildern sind ja auch eher traurige Anhängsel, ihrer eigentlichen Funktion beraubt. So wie ein letztes trauriges Winken der Potenz.

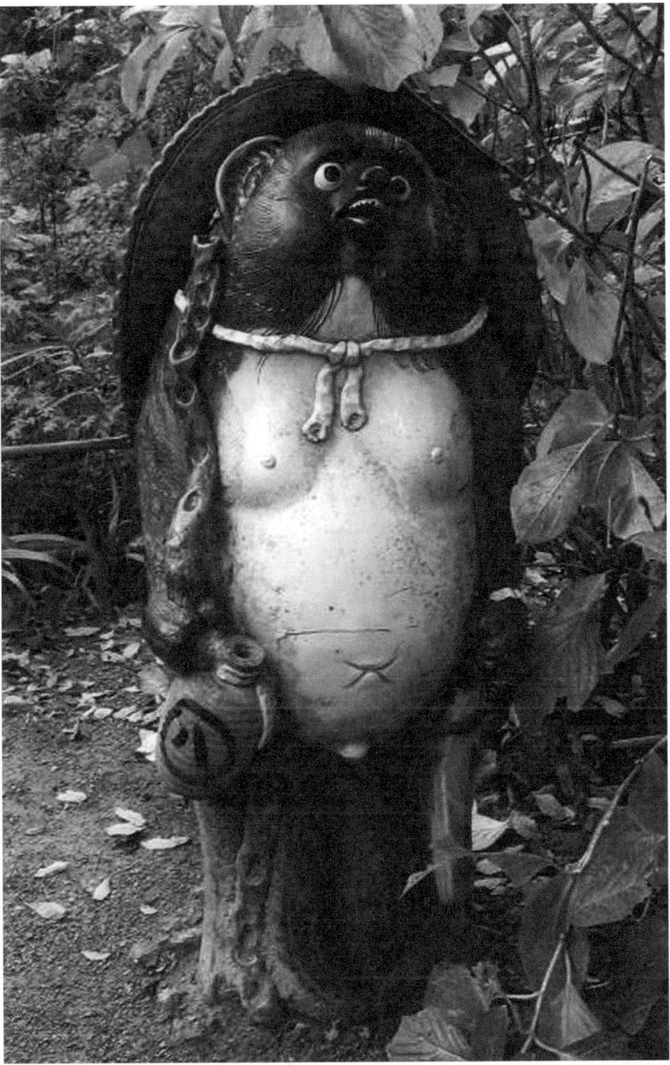

SP: Yes, I thought you'd like it. Something like the principle of panda versus grizzly bear. But this waving takes place in the knowledge of the massive baggage of the phallic symbol. What's nice about it is the multitude of possible associations, especially with a symbol that's so semantically one-dimensional. Or at best two-dimensional—for Lacan at least, the phallus is a dialectic symbol, since it unites the sublime of procreation with the profane of urination. So it's nice to be able to add a few more possibilities. In any case, we gallop right down the well-worn paths of cultural history, passing early stone sculptures and the giant members of ancient Greece, smiling at cravats, swords, and rockets, never leaving the realm of Freud, the Surrealists, Lacan, Theweleit...

MB: For me, these forms are also quite simply beautiful in painterly terms. One shouldn't forget that abstract form also plays a part. Added to which, all the associations linked with them are intended. One must be careful not to fall into these traps too often. It has to remain dynamic. And if these images are called to mind, I think the picture remains in such

Insofern sind sie unfreiwillig ein Gegenmodell.

Das wirkt ja nicht mehr angsteinflössend. Und dann doch eher wie bei deinen Tanuki, gemütlich. Es wird nicht mehr mit Penetration gedroht. Es wird eher gewunken. So als wollte man noch kurz darauf hinweisen, dass da mal etwas war. Und dann legt man sich lieber wieder aufs Bett.

Das Bild von einem Tanuki, der auf seinem ausgebreiteten Sack ruht gefällt mir sehr.

SP: Ja, das dachte ich mir, dass dir das gefällt. Sozusagen das Prinzip Panda- gegen Grizzleybär... Aber dieses Winken geschieht ja auch im Bewusstsein des Riesen-Gepäckstücks Phallussymbol.

Das Schöne daran ist ja die Vielzahl der möglichen Assoziationen, gerade bei einem seiner Art nach eher eindeutigen Symbol wie diesem. (Oder einem allerhöchstens zweideutigen..., bei Lacan zumindest ist der Phallus ein dialektisches Symbol, da er das Erhabene der Zeugung und das Profane des Pinkelns vereint. Da ist es doch schön, dem noch ein paar mehr Möglichkeiten hinzufügen zu können.)

Man rast jedenfalls direkt im Galopp über die plattgelatschten Pfade der Kulturgeschichte, frühzeitliche Steinskulpturen und die Riesenpimmel der griechischen Antike passierend, Krawatten, Schwerter, Raketen belächelnd, ist gleichzeitig bei Freud, den Surrealisten, Lacan, Theweleit...

MB: Für mich sind diese Formen auch malerisch einfach schön. Das darf man nicht vergessen, das spielt auch eine Rolle, die abstrakte Form. Und die ganzen Assoziationen, die daran hängen, sind ja gewollt. Man sollte aufpassen, nicht zu oft in diese Fallen zu tapsen. Es muss ja dynamisch bleiben. Und wenn diese Bilder im Kopf auftauchen, bleibt das Bild für mich beweglich.

Aber das stimmt schon, die Körpererfindungen in meinen Bildern befinden sich in einem Zustand der Transformation. Man kann die weiterspinnen. Wobei es auch einige gibt, die sich eher im Zustand des Einschlafens befinden. Da ist die Sache schon abgeschlossen. Ich denke da auch an Filmtrailer. Das, was im Kopf passiert, dieses Weiterspinnen eines Films, von dem man nur Bruchstücke kennt.

SP: Klaus Theweleit setzt alles Fliessende, alles Vermischte in die Nähe des Unbewussten. Flüsse, Fluten, Schlamm und Brei – alles Aggregatzustände, denen wir in der Bildwelt deiner Malerei ständig begegnen, sowohl inhaltlich / motivisch als auch formal, vom Farbauftrag her – sind für den soldatischen Mann (um den es ihm in Männerphantasien *geht), eine Bedrohung auf vielerlei Ebenen: Das Flüssige ist "... die grössere Formbarkeit, das noch*

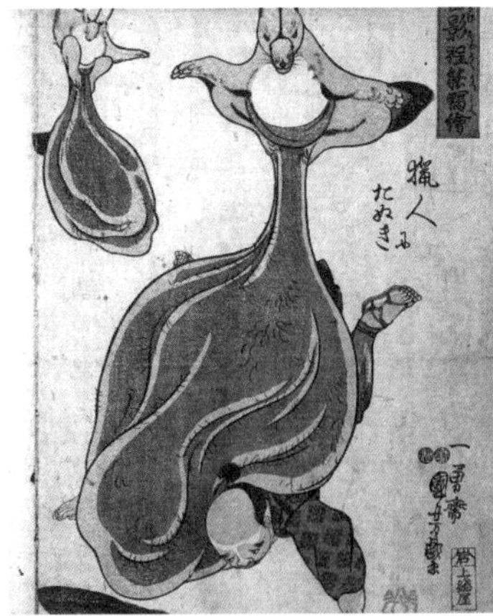

a dynamic state. But it is true, the physical sensations in my paintings are in a state of transformation. They can be taken further. Although there are some that are more in a state of falling asleep. The matter is already closed. I'm also thinking here of film trailers, what happens in your head, developing an idea of the whole film when you only know fragments.

SP: Klaus Theweleit associates all that flows and all that mingles with the unconscious. For the military man (about whom Theweleit is writing in *Male Fantasies*), rivers, floods, mire, pulp—all states that recur constantly in the pictorial world of your painting, both in terms of content and motif, and in formal and technical terms—present a threat on all kinds of levels: fluidity is equated with "the greater malleability and as yet unspent utopian potential of femaleness, a desiring-production that is fallow, undirected, not yet socially defined, and thus remains in closer proximity to the unconscious; a life of emotion, rather than intellect (that cruel, demarcating product of the constraints that beset men's bodies)..." The same applies to the floods inside the body; individuals experience their own innards as nothing but a heavy mass, as pulp. Which somehow brings us to the "mob" that often crops up in your titles.

MB: Initially, MOB was meant to be a title or designation of rank. Like in an army. The idea was that these figures are representatives of a collective or group.

SP: That would be quite an army of freaks. A bit like in movies about mercenaries. But doesn't the title also contain the idea of one figure being a group, a crowd, a riotous assembly, a mob? More than juxtaposition, there is superposition, muddle, and confusion in your figures. There is clearly an element of tumult and ruckus.

MB: In more recent works, that has changed somewhat. The figurations are now slightly simpler, more blatant. But of course you're right that the MOB in the title makes these figures multiple. And this tumult, as you call it, takes place within the figure. The figure is legion, so to speak. Like Satan, who always says "I am many."

SP: Right. And God says "I am what I am." You can't really argue with that.

MB: A hundred-member progressive rock band. An absurd musical collective. Or a sect. Something like Yahowa 13, with their leader Father Yod, who made music and recorded albums. That's a lovely and extremely touching idea, this unshakeable belief in the collective. We'll make love together, mathematically, and then music, sexually. Or we'll spend five years working on an album about the moon. The nice thing about such collectives is this urge to invent. To generate all manner of absurd concepts. That comes quite close to the way I approach painting. All my works are claims, too. Painterly inventions. Father Yod even invented planets. That's fabulous, that kind of artificiality. Cutting oneself off and deliberately withdrawing in order to see what else there is. I appreciate that. I think that's where some of the best things happen.

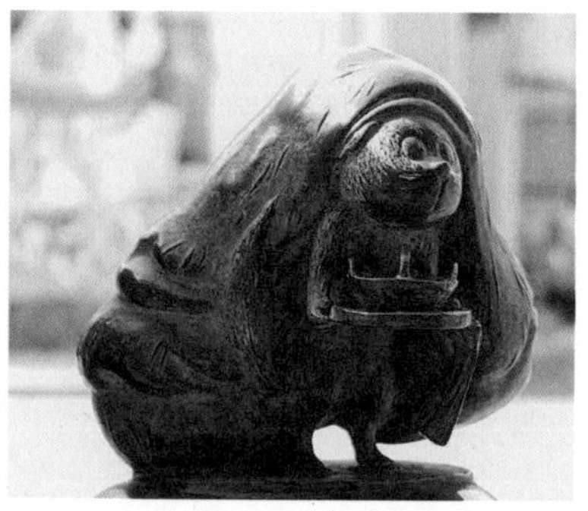

nicht vertane utopische Versprechen der Weiblichkeit, ihre noch nicht gesellschaftlich definierte ungerichtete, brachliegende Wunschproduktion und die damit gegebene grössere Nähe zum Unbewussten, ihr Leben in der Emotion statt im Intellekt, der ein grausames grenzziehendes Produkt der Eingrenzung ist, die den männlichen Körpern widerfuhr..."

Das gleiche gilt für die eigenen Körperfluten. Das Innere des Körpers wird vom Individuum unmittelbar nur als schwere Masse, als Brei wahrgenommen. Da sind wir dann ja auch irgendwie schon beim Mob, der in deinen Titeln immer wieder auftaucht...

MB: Der *MOB* war am Anfang als Titel- oder Rangbezeichnung gedacht. Wie in einer Armee. Es stand die Idee dahinter, dass diese Figuren Stellvertreter sind, für ein Kollektiv oder eine Gruppe.

SP: Das wäre dann ja eine ziemliche Freak-Armee. Ein bisschen so wie in Söldner-Filmen.

Aber steckt in dem Titel nicht auch die Idee einer Figur, die gleichzeitig Gruppe, Auflauf, Zusammenrottung, Mob ist? Innerhalb deiner Figuren findet ja auch weit mehr als ein Nebeneinander ein Übereinander, ein Drunter und Drüber und Durcheinander statt. Das hat eindeutig was von Tumult und Aufruhr.

MB: In den neueren Arbeiten hat sich das etwas geändert. Die Figurationen sind jetzt etwas einfacher, penetranter geworden.

Aber es stimmt natürlich, die Figur wird durch diesen MOB-Titel viele. Und dieser Tumult, wie du es nennst, spielt sich innerhalb der Figur ab. Die Figur ist sozusagen Legion. So wie Satan, der sagt ja auch immer "Ich bin viele".

SP: Stimmt. Und Gott sagt "Ich bin der ich bin". Da gibt's irgendwie nichts zu deuten.

MB: Eine 100-köpfige Progrock Band. So ein absurdes Musik-Kollektiv. Oder eine Sekte. So etwas wie Yahowa 13. Die haben ja mit ihrem Führer Father Yod auch Musik gemacht und Platten aufgenommen. Das ist eine schöne und extrem rührende Vorstellung, dieser unerschütterliche Glaube an das Kollektiv. Wir machen jetzt zusammen Liebe, mathematisch und danach Musik, sexuell. Oder 5 Jahre an einer LP über den Mond arbeiten.

Das schöne an solchen Kollektiven ist dieser Drang zur Erfindung. Zum Generieren von irgendwelchen absurden

SP: Another interesting thing about Yahowa 13 is the mixing. Not the mixing of oriental philosophy, New Age, Christianity, plus a bit of yoga, and Ra from the ancient Egyptians, etc, that's nothing new. But the fact that this happened in the middle of Hollywood. They all lived together in a huge villa in the Hollywood Hills and ran a successful vegetarian restaurant that was very popular with pop stars and actors. Also, untypically for a sect, the music is entirely in keeping with its time and place—California of the 1970s. Not just the obligatory mantras, but developing out of and contributing to western (psychedelic) pop. Not a turning away from reality, then, but more an embracing of it. Reality is transferred into a particular context and transformed, supplemented and perfected with distinctive and peculiar elements. Yahowa 13 were also very theatrical, and it seems they were all involved, which is nice, as the more usual version is that followers are exploited as props for the gurus own self-presentation.

MB: It's also nice that this spectacle ended not with collective suicide but in a perfectly modern manner when Father Yod died hang-gliding. That rounds the picture off very well.

That was strange, that picture of the over-adorned Bulgarian bride you sent me. And diabolically sad, too. In this case, it's an almost violent act. The bride is barely recognizable, she's been turned into a gigantic bouquet of flowers. She becomes a sculpture. Decorated to death, so to speak. Which is also something I've often done with my figures. All you see is an eye or a tooth or some other thing that suggests a face. And I always tell myself that this is a nice trap. If there's an eye, the picture of a figure immediately comes to mind. Which is wonderfully simple and stupid. I once quite dumbly included clocks in some pictures—a totally overloaded symbol, mostly painted into a Napoleon hat. And then someone actually wrote something about time passing and life slipping past. That was great. I was thinking more about the silliest way of getting the concept of time into a picture. You paint a clock. Added to which, it was a bit like Flavor Flav's clock, the giant one he always wears round his neck.

SP: Ah, Flavor Flav! He too has now become a tragicomic figure. In the MTV programme *Flavor of Love*, he selects a bride from a group of exquisitely fucked-up, crazy women. Every week, one gets sent home: "Your time is up." And if you make it to the next round: "You know what time it is, baby." And the women get the huge clocks hung round their necks, like the cheap gold necklaces they awarded on *The Bachelor*. That's a similar approach to symbolism as what you're describing. Now there's also Rock of Love with Bret Michaels from Poison. The same thing, just with rock bitches instead of ghetto bitches. And the doorway to the next round is: "Will you stay and rock my world?" I like to watch that. In a sense, what goes on there is like school summer camp. Totally staged and planned, of course—tumult and rivalry and cabin fever are expected and provoked. But in any case, it's certainly another example of a mob.

MB: And it's strange how a symbol like this, which Public Enemy initially used in a very political sense, nothing to do with

Konzepten. Das kommt dem Vorgang meiner Malerei ziemlich nahe. Das sind ja auch alles Behauptungen. Malerei-Erfindungen eben. Father Yod hat ja sogar Planeten erfunden. Das ist doch traumhaft. Diese Art der Künstlichkeit. Dieses sich abkoppeln und sich bewusst zurückziehen, um dann zu schauen was es noch gibt. Das schätze ich. Ich glaube mit die besten Sachen passieren da.

SP: Spannend an Yahowa 13 ist ja auch die Durchmischung. Nicht die Durchmischung von östlicher Philosophie, Esoterik, Christentum, dann noch ein bisschen Yoga und Ra von den alten Ägyptern usw., das kennt man ja. Aber dass das dann mitten in Hollywood stattgefunden hat, die wohnten ja alle zusammen in einer riesigen Villa in den Hills. Und betrieben ein bei Popstars und Schauspielern sehr beliebtes und erfolgreiches vegetarisches Restaurant.

Auch die Musik ist (ganz Sekten-untypisch) voll in ihrer Zeit und ihrem Ort, nämlich dem Kalifornien der 1970er, verortet. Eben nicht nur obligatorische Mantra-Rezitation, sondern entspringend aus und Beitrag zum westlichen (Psychedelic) Pop. Also nicht Abkehr, sondern eher Umarmung der Wirklichkeit. Die wird in den eigenen Kontext aufgenommen und umge-

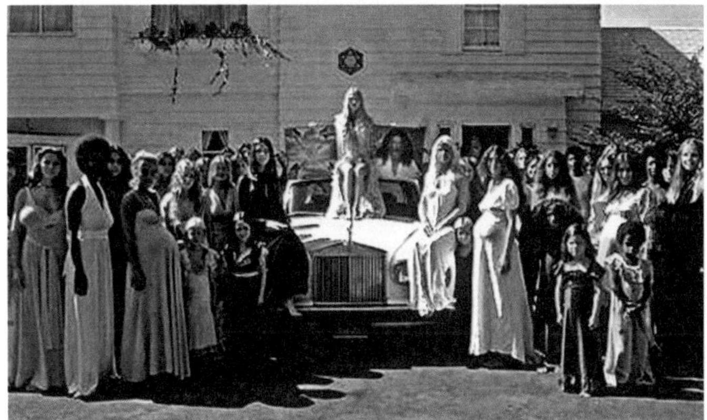

wandelt, durch das Eigene und Eigenartige ergänzt, um sie zu vervollkommnen.

Die hatten ja auch unheimlichen Spass an der Inszenierung und waren anscheinend auch alle daran beteiligt. Was schön ist, da man das ja eigentlich eher so kennt, dass die Anhänger für die Inszenierung eines Gurus instrumentalisiert werden.

MB: Schön war ja auch, dass diese Inszenierung nicht mit einem kollektiven Selbstmord endete sondern ganz modern damit, dass Father Yod beim Gleitschirmfliegen ums Leben kam. Das rundet das Bild ja auch gut ab.

Das war merkwürdig, dieses Bild der zugeschmückten bulgarischen Braut, das du mir geschickt hast. Auch ein teuflisch trauriges Bild. Wobei das ja in diesem Falle ein fast schon gewalttätiger Akt ist. Die Braut ist gar nicht mehr zu erkennen, die ist in einen riesigen Blumenstrauss verwandelt worden. Die wird zur Skulptur. Totgeschmückt sozusagen. Das hab ich auch oft mit meinen Figuren gemacht. Da sieht man auch nur noch ein Auge oder einen Zahn oder halt irgendetwas, das auf ein Gesicht hindeutet. Wobei ich mir

SP: The many borders and frames in your pictures also function like plinths. They seem to point again and again to the fact that these are pictures. As if they were insisting on their own artificiality.

MB: Yes. Also the crossing out in the new pictures with green

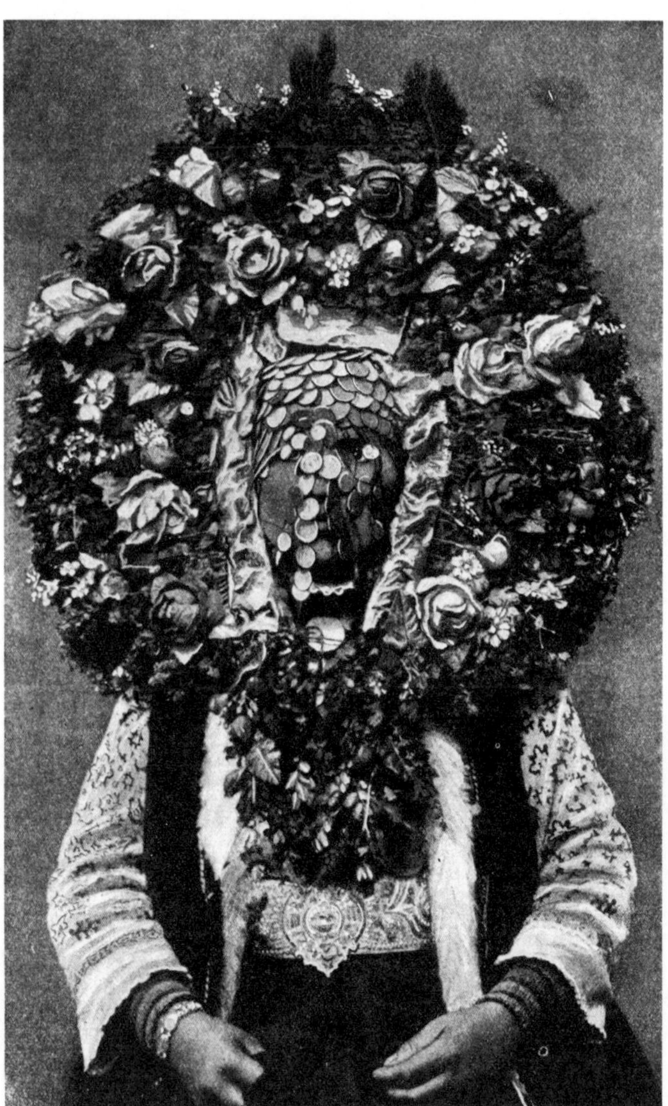

immer sage, das ist ja auch eine schöne Falle. Wenn da ein Auge ist, hast du sofort das Bild einer Figur im Kopf. Das ist wunderbar einfach und dumm.

Ich hab mal Uhren, also ein völlig überladenes Symbol, so ganz doof in die Bilder gemalt. Meistens in einen Napoleon-Hut. Und dann hat einer tatsächlich mal etwas über die ablaufende Lebenszeit geschrieben. Das war toll. Ich dachte eher daran, was ist die dämlichste Art und Weise, den Begriff Zeit in ein Bild zu bekommen. Man malt eine Uhr. Ausserdem hatte die auch etwas von Flavour Flavs Uhr. Dieses Riesenteil, das er immer umhängen hat.

SP: Ach, der Flavour Flav! Auch inzwischen eine tragikomische Figur. Die MTV Sendung, Flavour of Love, *in der er sich aus einer Auswahl von exquisit abgefuckten, durchgeknallten Frauen eine Braut aussucht. Jede Woche wird eine nach Hause geschickt: "Your time is up". Eine Runde weiter: "You know what time it is, baby" und die Frauen kriegen die riesigen Uhren umgehängt wie damals beim* Bachelor *die Tschibokettchen. Das ist ein ähnlicher Umgang mit Symbolik wie du ihn beschreibst.*

Mittlerweile gibt es auch Rock of Love *mit Bret Michaels von Poison. Das gleiche, nur eben keine Ghetto- sondern Rockbitches. Eine Runde weiter = "Will you stay and rock my world?" Gucke ich sehr gern. Das ist ja in gewisser Weise Schullandheim, was da passiert. Natürlich komplett inszeniert und durchgeplant, Aufruhr, Konkurrenzkampf, Lagerkoller werden erwartet und provoziert. Und doch haben wir es auf alle Fälle wieder mit einem Mob zu tun...*

MB: Es ist natürlich auch merkwürdig wie sich so ein Symbol, das ja am Anfang von Public Enemy ein durch und durch politisches war, also nicht Bling Bling, wie sich das auf einmal umwandelt.

Wenn man sich so eine Szene anschaut, dann merkt man, dass das Bild eigentlich eingefroren ist in dem Moment, in dem die Rose oder das Kettchen oder die Uhr überreicht wird. Und Flavour Flav oder Brett Michaels werden zur Skulptur. Mit einer Geste, die ins Nichts führt. Dieses Ritual der Auszeichnung.

Das geht meinen Skulpturen ja ähnlich. *DJ Penize* z.B. besteht aus 3 Sockeln. Der erste Sockel trägt die Figur, die Figur ist Sockel für den Kugelschreiber und dieser ist ein Sockel für die Kontaktdaten meines Steuerberaters. Und die werden da am Ende überreicht. Das ist so als würde die Skulptur eine Rose überreichen mit den Worten: "Will you stay and rock my world?". Das ist dasselbe Muster, würde ich sagen.

Am Ende des Rituals wird man dann doch enttäuscht.

SP: Die zahlreichen Borden und Rahmen in deinen Bildern funktionieren ja auch ähnlich wie Sockel. Sie scheinen immer wieder darauf hinweisen zu wollen, dass es sich bei ihnen um Bilder handelt. So als ob sie auf ihre eigene Künstlichkeit bestehen würden.

MB: Ja. Auch das Durchstreichen in den neuen Bildern, mit der grünen Schultafelfarbe.
Das Gute daran ist, dass es das Bild zurück in die Malerei

blackboard paint. The good thing about this is that it reclaims the picture for painting, away from illusionism and towards a flyer or poster. Towards abstraction, then, and away from storytelling. The pictures are meant to jump back and forth between these two poles. This generates movement. Looking at these pictures now I'm also reminded of the scene in The Omen *where the photographer discovers the light effects in his pictures, harbingers of a fiendish accident; the priest, who is later impaled on a church steeple. I like it when such images occur to me belatedly. There is an anecdote about Baselitz showing Johannes Gachnang new works that all had a very particular pattern. And Gachnang was in his studio and noticed some Italian matchboxes and said: "Oh I see, you're painting Italian matchboxes." I like that. Things that are lying at your feet the whole time. You just don't notice how certain things find their way into your pictures. It's rather a stupid feeling. But that can only be good. One should accept it all, this unconscious material. It's something you can usually trust. And it joins everything else in the whole baggage of painting—which is already brimming over, and that can become a problem.*

SP: But it's also a huge resource, a great playground where you can go wild.

MB: Yes, of course, and that resource is exploited to the full. Sometimes consciously and sometimes unconsciously. And this also obeys its own logic and grammar. But sometimes it's also important to examine this resource with authoritarian, dictatorial instruments, like a set of rules or a filter. Not just wandering round the supermarket taking everything that's on offer.

SP: What I see in your work above all is that you devise highly distinctive pictorial worlds and let them develop their own inner tension. By which I mean that within the picture, the hat might make fun of the penis, or vice versa, instead of you as the artist imposing your view on us. You create your own system and trust it to explain itself on its own terms. Or not, as the case may be.

MB: It's fine for the picture to talk to itself, to keep rummaging through itself, like in a washing machine.

SP: Flavor Flav's clocks, fantasy sex organs, decorated with little hats and feathers and flooded by pulp, diligently coloured -in patterns next to areas of paint applied with great gusto whose elegance and sensuality are derived entirely from their materiality: all this taken together is a flexible system, things get mixed up—the profane with the sublime, the familiar with the totally strange, going so far that such distinctions are no longer identifiable. It's like an alchemical balancing act. And the rummaging and recycling is never the point of departure or the driving force, but always a supplement and complement to what you've invented yourself.

Your work is also a real celebration of enjoyment, elegance, and sensuality. And of the sexiness of the materiality of paint, although without relying on this exclusively, without expecting that to "work" on its own. The result is an extravagant beauty

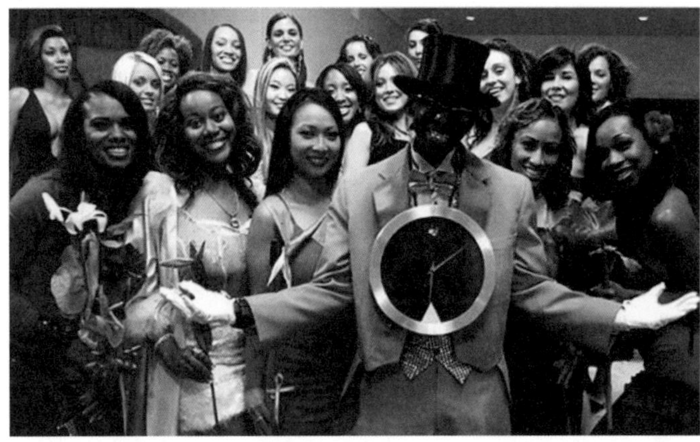

holt, weg vom Illusionistischen und hin zum Flyer oder zum Poster. Also hin zur Abstraktion und weg von der Geschichte. Die Bilder sollen ja zwischen diesen Polen hin und her springen. Dann kommt Bewegung ins Spiel.

Wenn ich diese Bilder jetzt sehe, denke ich an diese Szene in *Das Omen*, in der der Fotograf auf seinen Bildern diese Lichtstreifen entdeckt, Vorboten eines teuflischen Unfalls. Der Pfarrer, der dann später von einer Kirchturmspitze durchbohrt wird.

Das finde ich schön, wenn solche Bilder mir dann mit Verspätung einfallen. Es gibt da diese Anekdote, in der Baselitz Johannes Gachnang seine neuen Arbeiten zeigt, die alle so ein ganz spezielles Muster haben. Und Gachnang ist im Atelier und entdeckt diese italienischen Streichholzschachteln und meint nur: Aha, du malst also italienische Streichholzschachteln. Das mag ich. Dinge, die die ganze Zeit vor deinen Füssen liegen. Und man merkt gar nicht, wie sich bestimmte Sachen dann in die Bilder schleichen. Da kommt man sich schon etwas dumm vor. Aber das ist ja nur gut, das sollte man alles zulassen. Dieses Unbewusste. Dem kann man meistens gut vertrauen.

Das kommt dann auch mit hinein in den ganzen Rucksack Malerei. Der ist randvoll und das kann sich auch zum Problem entwickeln.

SP: Das ist aber doch auch ein riesiger Fundus... Da kann man sich doch wunderbar austoben.

MB: Ja sicher, der wird ja auch ausgeschöpft. Mal bewusst und mal unbewusst. Und dieses Unbewusste folgt ja auch seiner eigenen Logik und Grammatik. Aber dieser Fundus muss zuweilen auch mit autoritären, diktatorischen Instrumenten untersucht werden. Ein Regelwerk oder einen Filter dazwischen schalten. Also nicht durch den Supermarkt latschend alles mitnehmen, was da so herumliegt.

SP: Was ich bei dir vor allem sehe, ist, dass du ganz eigene Bilderwelten entwickelst und diese ihre Spannung aus sich selbst beziehen lässt. Ich meine damit, dass sich dann vielleicht innerhalb des Bildes z.B. das Hütchen über das Pimmelchen lustig macht oder auch umgekehrt, anstatt dass du als Künstler uns deinen Blick diktierst. Du schaffst dein eigenes System

that embraces deformation and leans in all directions, overflowing into the ridiculous, the grotesque, the tragic, like your sculptures overflowing their plinths. Or like the Bulgarian bride.

MB: Yes, all that is welcome in the picture. And the pathos that's always there as soon as one starts doing painting. The soft clock, the lonely painter, the severed ear, etcetera. All of which is great material. As well as this sometimes really peculiar feeling of being a painter when one is struggling through ornaments. Work in the studio in general. As if I was mixing my own paint with egg whites and rabbit-skin glue. Like at the academy I attended, in some of the painting classes. People who spent two months painting a damn vase or an old horse. Layer on layer, with tired eyes and candlelight in front of the easel. Until late at night. Always in the knowledge that: Yes, I am a painter. And then, the next day, the professor came and declared in a grouchy voice: "No! You're not a painter yet! Not yet!" I found this pathos very sad, but also very entertaining. There they all were, up in the attic, painting themselves literally crazy. And I don't want to say anything against that. They meant it seriously. When I spend three hours colouring in little squares, I get a taste of that sadness. It's not a bad thing to subject oneself to now and then.

But there is something in painting that I can't experience in this form anywhere else. It's complicated and I can't describe it precisely. But it has a magic all of its own.

SP: I think this magic, as you call it, has a great deal to do with the materiality of the medium. And with the process by which the painting emerges.

MB: Maybe it has to do with the fact that painting always places several levels of time over one another, past and present and future. Everything is there at the same time. And a good picture always continues painting itself, either forwards towards tomorrow, or backwards towards the starting point. To zero, so to speak.

SP: While we're on the subject of magic: with Robert Kraiss and Florian Gass, you play in the *Ylmaz House Band*. I would describe your music as some kind of gamelan drone, both reduced and out-of-hand at the same time. Drone has a fluid-swampy emotional quality to it—which brings us back to pulp. The pulse of drone is less a heartbeat than the undulating sensation of blood flowing in the veins or perhaps the activity of the digestive tract. And then there's your singing, which comes from deep inside and sounds like it could only be made by totally switching off the thinking machine and relaxing every muscle. Like the unconscious rendered into sound. Or the free-flowing inner pulp.

There's also clearly an element of ritual here. Comparisons with music from Asia and Africa are problematic, as it might sound like you're drawing on that and cobbling your music together à la world music. That's not the case. But the influence is clearly audible. One similarity with the gamelan is the alternation between quite reduced moments and passages of chaos, both of which naturally arise from the same order. Maybe it's

und traust dem auch zu, dass es sich aus sich selbst erklärt oder auch nicht.

MB: Das Bild soll ruhig mit sich selber reden, sich immer wieder durchwühlen, wie in einer Waschmaschine.

SP: Flavor Flavs Uhren, fantastische Geschlechtsteile, mit Hütchen und Federn geschmückt und von Brei überschwemmt, fleissig ausgepinselte Muster neben genussvoll aufgetragenen Farbpartien, die ihre Eleganz und Sinnlichkeit ganz aus ihrer Materialität speisen... Das ist insgesamt ein bewegliches System, es gibt Vermischungszustände – des Profanen mit dem Sublimen, des Vertrauten mit dem ganz und gar Merkwürdigen, soweit, dass man solche Unterscheidungen gar nicht mehr machen kann... Das ist auch wie ein alchemistisches Ausbalancieren. Und der Griff in die Mottenkiste ist nie Ausgangspunkt oder Motor, sondern immer Ergänzung und Vervollkommnung der eigenen Erfindung.

Deine Arbeit ist auch ein regelrechtes Abfeiern von Genuss, Eleganz und Sinnlichkeit. Und auch von der Sexiness der Materialität der Farbe, ohne sich allein darauf zu verlassen, also ohne die Erwartung, dass das "funktioniert". Resultat ist eine überbordende, die Deformation umarmende Schönheit, die zu allen Seiten kippt, ins Lächerliche, Groteske, Tragische überschwappt, wie deine Skulpturen über ihre Sockel. Oder wie die bulgarische Braut.

MB: Ja, das kann alles ins Bild hinein. Und auch das Pathos, das da immer mitschwingt, sobald man Malerei betreibt. Die weiche Uhr, der einsame Maler, das abgeschnittene Ohr usw. Das ist ja auch grossartiges Material. Auch dieses manchmal wirklich sonderbare Gefühl Maler zu sein..., wenn man sich durch so blöde Ornamente quält. Überhaupt, die Arbeit im Atelier. Als würde ich mir mit Ei und Hasenleim die Farben anmischen. Sowie an der Akademie, auf der ich war, in einigen Malerklassen. Leute, die 2 Monate damit beschäftigt waren eine verdammte Vase oder einen Ackergaul zu malen. Schicht für Schicht, mit müden Augen und Kerzenlicht vor der Staffelei. Bis tief in die Nacht. Immer wissend, ja ich bin Maler. Und dann kam am nächsten Tag der Professor und hat mit Brummbärenstimme verkündet: "Nein! Noch bist du kein Maler! Noch nicht!" Dieses Pathos fand ich sehr traurig aber auch sehr unterhaltsam. Die hingen da alle unterm Dach und haben sich regelrecht um den Verstand gemalt. Da will ich auch gar nichts gegen sagen. Die haben es ja ernst gemeint. Naja und wenn ich drei Stunden Kästchen ausmale bekomme ich einen Geschmack dieser Tristesse. Das kann man sich ja ab und an auch mal antun.

Und dennoch ist da etwas in der Malerei, was ich nirgendwo sonst so erfahren kann. Das ist kompliziert, ich kann das auch nicht genau beschreiben. Aber da gibt es schon eine ganz eigene Magie.

SP: Diese Magie, wie du es nennst, hat viel mit der Materialität der Malerei zu tun, denke ich. Und mit ihrem Entstehungsprozess.

MB: Vielleicht hat es zu tun mit der Tatsache, dass die Malerei

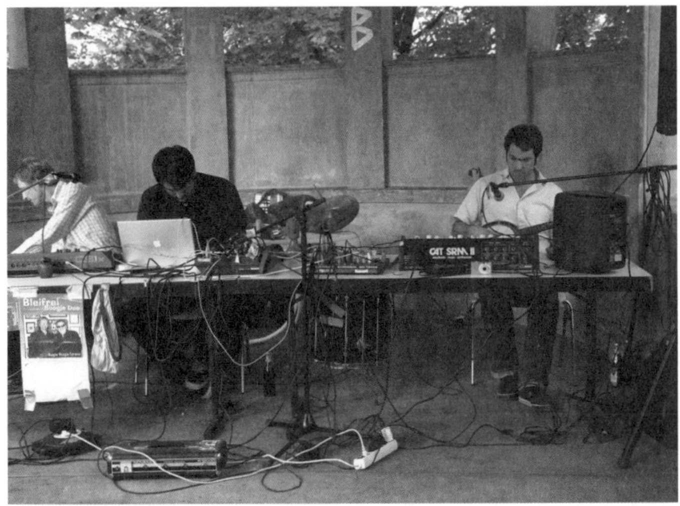

also the feeling of being present at a ritual. As if, in addition to the artist and the work, the presence of a third element is assumed. It might be the spirit of nature, as in an animist ritual. Or the gods, or God. Or something completely different, even if it's just the phantom being that's created when you make something together as a group. As I see it, you create this feeling above all by means of reduction. And by repetition and the ceasing of repetition, the gap. That makes room for the third presence, so to speak.

MB: This third being is not only present, it also shapes and completes the process. There is the theory of the Third Body that takes shape between the source and the listener when music is played. But maybe that's going too far.

SP: When looking at your pictures I'm often reminded of non-European art, although, as in the case of the phallus symbol, I'm also thinking in terms of its use in the context of—among others—Modernism. At the same time, it makes me think of photographs of indigenous peoples, especially the pictures from colonial times in which the people are served up on a plate just like your figures.

MB: The way I look at the figures can certainly be compared with this colonial gaze. They're portraits, of course. And they all end up in the archive. For a while my pictures also featured strictly symmetrical compositions. That also had an element of obsessive collecting and cataloging. The result was a family tree, a chronicle. And I can play around with making links, establishing hierarchies. It's a very childish approach. Taken together, the pictures make up something like an army, or a system that's constantly being extended. Or a large tea party coming together. In my head I use them like actors. Which is fun, as it fosters a healthy distance to the pictures if you use them as playing cards. Then I begin to see the pictures as posters or flyers. I've always liked that. It means I have my own banana republic.

SP: Can you explain the idea of the cinema trailer again?

immer mehrere Zeitenebenen übereinander legt, Vergangenheit und Gegenwart und Zukunft. Alles ist gleichzeitig vorhanden. Und ein gutes Bild malt sich selbst immer weiter, entweder nach vorne in Richtung morgen, oder nach hinten, zum Ausgangspunkt. Zum Nullpunkt sozusagen.

SP: Wo wir gerade bei Magie sind: Du bist zusammen mit Robert Kraiss und Florian Gass die Ylmaz House Band. Eure Musik würde ich jetzt mal als eine Art gleichzeitig reduzierten und ausufernden Gamelan-Drone bezeichnen.

Drone hat ja auch so eine flüssig-sumpfige Gefühlsqualität – da sind wir wieder beim Brei. Der Puls des Drone ist weniger Herzschlag als das wabernde Gefühl des Blutstroms in den Adern oder vielleicht der Verdauung im Darm.

Dazu euer Gesang, der kommt von ganz tief drinnen und hört sich an, als könne er nur entstehen, wenn die Denkmaschine komplett gestoppt und alle Muskeln locker gelassen werden. Wie das Klang gewordene Unbewusste. Oder der frei fliessende innere Brei.

Das hat auch ganz klar etwas von Ritual. Verweise auf Musik aus Asien und Afrika sind eher schwierig, weil das vielleicht so klingt, als würdet ihr euch dort bedienen und das à la Weltmusik zusammenbasteln. So ist es ja nicht. Aber der Einfluss ist schon deutlich hörbar. Dem Gamelan ähnlich ist z.B. der Wechsel zwischen ganz reduzierten Momenten und Passagen des Chaos, welche natürlich beide der gleichen Ordnung entspringen.

Vielleicht ist es auch das Gefühl, einem Ritual beizuwohnen. Als ob zusätzlich zu Künstler und Werk noch etwas Drittes als anwesend vorausgesetzt wird. Das kann natürlich wie im animistischen Ritual die beseelte Natur sein. Oder die Götter oder Gott. Oder etwas komplett anderes, sei es nur das Geistwesen, das entsteht, wenn ihr als Gruppe zusammen etwas schafft.

Ich denke, dieses Gefühl erzeugt ihr vor allem mit Reduktion. Und durch Wiederholung und das Aussetzen der Wiederholung, die Lücke. Das gibt dann sozusagen Platz für das Drittwesen.

MB: Dieses Drittwesen ist nicht nur anwesend, es formt und vervollständigt auch den Prozess. Es gibt ja die Theorie des Dritten Körpers, der beim Hören von Musik zwischen Empfänger und Sender entsteht. Aber das führt jetzt vielleicht zu weit.

SP: Ich muss bei deinen Bildern schon auch oft an aussereuropäische Kunst denken, wobei ich dann, ähnlich wie beim Thema Phallussymbol, ja auch wieder deren Verwertung in der Moderne z.B. im Kopf hab. Gleichzeitig denke ich auch an Fotografien von Naturvölkern, vor allem an diese kolonialzeitlichen Aufnahmen, auf denen die Leute genauso auf dem Präsentierteller stehen wie deine Figuren.

MB: Meinen Blick auf die Figuren kann man durchaus vergleichen mit diesem kolonialistischen Blick. Das sind natürlich Portraits. Und die kommen dann alle ins Archiv. Eine Zeit lang waren die Bilder ja auch sehr streng symmetrisch angelegt.

Das hat auch etwas von Sammlerwut und Katalogisierung. Da ensteht ein Stammbaum, eine Familienchronik. Und ich kann dann damit spielen, Verbindungen herstellen, Hierarchien aufbauen.

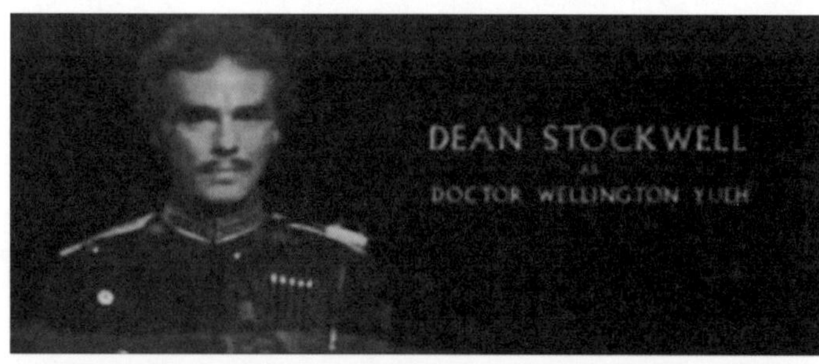

SP: This aspect, which I would call meditative, is essential for
me, both in approaching art and while working. This strong
focus that allows one to think of nothing or to actually not
think, I find this one of the best moments when working. It's
actually yoga. If it doesn't happen on its own, I can also evoke
this state quite well by listening to music. Best of all with

Das ist eine ganz kindliche Herangehensweise. Alle Bilder
zusammen bilden so etwas wie eine Armee, oder ein System,
das sich ständig erweitert. Das ist eine stattliche Kaffeetafel,
die man da zusammen bekommt. Im Kopf benutze ich sie wie
Schauspieler. Das macht Freude. Da ensteht auch eine ge-
sunde Distanz zu den Bildern, wenn man sie so benutzt. Wie
Spielkarten. Dann werden die Bilder für mich zu Postern oder
Flyern. Das hat mir immer gut gefallen. Ich hab dann meine
eigene Bananenrepublik.

MB: Wenn ich über Ausstellungen nachdenke, wie ich da heran
gehe, dann hab oft ich diesen Abspann von Dune im Kopf. Der
Abspann ist so ziemlich das Grossartigste an dem ganzen Film.
Man sieht das Meer und es werden nach und nach die einzelnen
Protagonisten des Filmes sowie Schauspieler und Rollenname
eingeblendet. Und dazu hört man eine Musik von Toto. Das ist
wie nach einer Theateraufführung, wenn alle nochmal auf die
Bühne kommen. Wirklich sehr theatralisch. Ich kann das nicht
genau erklären, aber das hat mich, als ich den Film als Teen-
ager gesehen habe, fasziniert. Mehr als der Film selbst.

Am liebsten würde ich einfach nur einen Film zeigen, in dem
meine Bilder kurz hintereinander erscheinen.

Eine Diashow. Das wäre eine elegante Lösung. Mit den da-
zugehörigen Titeln und einer Archivnummer.

Der Dune Abspann ist ja eher so etwas wie das stolze Aufzei-
gen von Erfindungen. Der Schmetterlingssammler, der die
besten Exemplare der Öffentlichkeit präsentiert. Der Trailer
hat ja eine andere Aufgabe, die aber für mich auch mit meinen
Arbeiten zu tun hat. Fand ich auch super als Kind. Man sieht so
etwas und hat dann tausend Bilder mehr im Kopf. Piranja, der
war extrem gut. Und Jaws. So ein Trailer ist ja auch erstmal
nur eine Behauptung. Und damit ein Versprechen auf etwas
Grossartiges, Aufregendes. Das ist wie Malerei. Und dieses Versprechen kann man ruhig ab und an brechen. Dann bleibt die
Uhr im Hut eben doch nur ein Witz.

Dieses Teasen kann man auch sehr gut in der Malerei an-
wenden. Lockstoffe, falsche Fährten, in Sicherheit wiegen. Und
vor allem geht es dabei in erster Linie um mich und nicht den
Betrachter. Dieses in Fallen laufen, das will ich selbst beim
Malen erleben. Ich mach es manchmal z.B. so, dass ich mich
bei einem grossen Bild tagelang nur mit einer kleinen Stelle
beschäftige. Als hätte ich Scheuklappen auf. Tunnelblickmalen.
Erstens dient das dem eigenen Entertainment. Und zweitens
dem Bild. So einen Fokus anzuwenden und das Bild als ganzes
auszublenden ist wichtig. Wenn man die ganze Zeit das fertige
Bild wie eine Mohrrübe vorm Kopf baumeln hat, wird man oft
zu schnell. Man hat's dann eilig. Und eh man sich versieht ist
das Ding fertig.

Etwas, was wir übrigens bei den der Ylmaz House Band oft an-
wenden. Das Komische ist, wenn wir unsere Aufnahmen später
anhören, ist dieser Fokus, dieses Ausblenden kaum noch wahr-
zunehmen. Es fügt sich dann doch immer irgendwie zusammen.

Terry Riley and his *Dervishes* recordings. Him, the electric organ, and a delay, and you drift off. An "orchestra of one" that manages to make celestial music. You really get the feeling of something divine in art! I saw him this year in Los Angeles at the gigantic wooden organ in the Walt Disney Concert Hall. It was amazing. He came in, took off his shoes, and vanished in his socks among the forest of over six thousand organ pipes—which he calls *"Hurricane Mama"* as an alternative to the mocking title of *"French Fries"* that refers to the organ's appearance—and he really does unleash something like an emotional hurricane. Absolutely overwhelming. And without being at all pompous—not like *Carmina Burana*. I had tears in my eyes more than once.

Terry Riley has also made sound recordings of planets and turned them into pieces of music. Which reminds me of your hundred-member prog-rock band, or even six thousand members. Or maybe not. Eight-minute flute solos often bring one crashing back to earth. It's impossible to lose yourself in that because the artistic will is such a tangible presence. The opposite of the positively celestial "orchestra of one" would be the kind of one-man band you see busking in the street, with a bass drum on his back, and a tambourine on his head, condemned to always have one foot in the realm of the ridiculous. In your work, both these elements are present, including the whole jumble of possible emotional reactions to them. And as a painter who creates a whole mob, you're a kind of one-man orchestra, too, vanishing into your own forest of organ pipes or under a heap of homemade instruments, as you please.

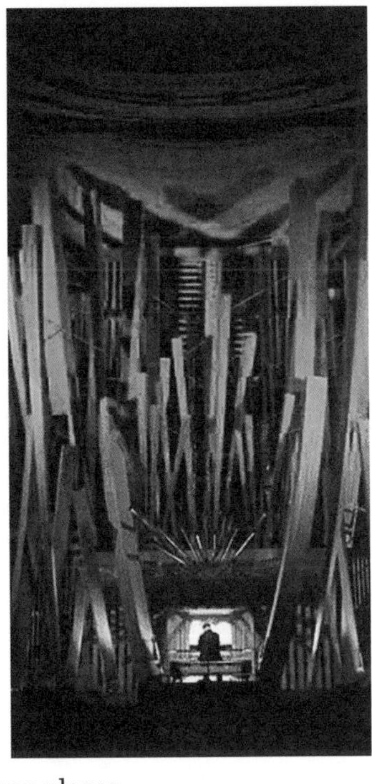

MB: Yes, I don't want to be visible in the pictures at all. That would be awful. I prefer to send out a troop of mutants—and be responsible for the formations, for deployment and strategy. But there's certainly no place for me in the pictures themselves. When I first showed the sculptures, I had the idea that I wanted Florian Gass to be somehow part of the exhibition. So it was the whole Ylmaz House Band, as Robert Kraiss was showing his pictures in the next room. When it came to naming the sculptures, I thought we can just use the best of the DJ names we once dreamed up for Florian: DJ Penize, DJ Penny Denny B., etcetera. It had nothing to do with my individual sculptures. But it was nice that I pressed them into this representative role. And then I had my banana republic again.

Stefanie Popp is an artist and lives in Cologne.

geradezu unverzichtbar, sowohl beim Herangehen an Kunst als auch beim Arbeiten selbst. Dieser starke Focus, durch den es auch passiert, dass man an nichts oder tatsächlich nicht denkt, das gehört zu den schönsten Momenten beim Arbeiten, finde ich. Das ist ja eigentlich Yoga.

Wenn das von selber nicht passiert, kann ich diesen Zustand auch ganz gut mit Musikhören erzeugen. Am besten mit Terry Riley und seinen Dervishes-Aufnahmen. Er, die elektrische Orgel und ein Delay und du hebst ab. Ein "Orchestra of one", das es fertig bringt, überirdische Musik zu erzeugen. Da kommt wirklich das Gefühl von etwas Göttlichem in der Kunst auf!

Ich habe ihn dieses Jahr in Los Angeles an der hölzernen Riesenorgel der Walt Disney Concert Hall gesehen. Das war Wahnsinn. Er kommt rein, zieht seine Schuhe aus, und verschwindet auf Söckchen in den Wald aus über 6000 Orgelpfeifen, die er als Gegenmodell zur "Pommestüte", als die die Orgel wegen ihres Aussehens verspottet wird, "Hurricane Mama" getauft hat, und entfacht echt so etwas wie einen emotionalen Hurrican. Absolut überwältigend. Dabei ganz ohne pompös zu sein, nix Carmina Burana. Mir kamen mehrmals die Tränen.

Terry Riley hat ja auch Tonaufnahmen von Planeten und daraus Musikstücke gemacht.

Was mich natürlich wieder an deine 100-köpfige, oder besser 6000-köpfige Progrock Band erinnert. Oder eben gerade nicht. Das achtminütige Flötensolo bringt einen ja oft sehr schnell zum Boden der Tatsachen zurück. Darin kann man sich gar nicht verlieren, weil man das Wollen so stark spürt.

Gegenpart zu dem geradezu überirdischen "Orchestra of one" wäre ja die Ein-Mann-Kapelle aus der Fussgängerzone, mit Bassdrum hintendrauf und Tambourin auf dem Kopf. Verdammt dazu, immer mit einem Fuss in der Lächerlichkeit zu stehen. In deiner Arbeit ist beides zu finden, inklusive des ganzen Wusts an emotionalen Reaktionsmöglichkeiten darauf.

Und als Maler, der einen ganzen Mob erschafft, bist du ja auch irgendwie so eine Art Ein-Mann-Orchester und verschwindest in deinem eigenen Orgelpfeifenwald oder auch unter einem Haufen von selbstgebastelten Instrumenten, je nach Belieben...

MB: Ja, ich will da ja auch überhaupt nicht sichtbar sein in den Bildern. Das wäre furchtbar. Ich schick doch dann lieber eine Mutantentruppe vor. Ich bin dann zuständig für die Formationen, für die Aufstellung und die Strategien. Aber in den Bildern selbst hab ich nichts verloren.

Als ich die ersten Skulpturen gezeigt habe, da war eine Überlegung, dass ich Florian Gass auch irgendwie in der Ausstellung haben wollte. Also die gesamte Ylmaz House Band. Robert Kraiss hat ja seine Bilder im Raum nebenan gezeigt. Und als es um die Titel für die Skulpturen ging, dachte ich mir, wir nehmen einfach die besten DJ Namen, die wir uns für Florian mal ausgedacht hatten. DJ Penize, DJ Pennydenny B. usw. Das hatte gar nichts mit den einzelnen Skulpturen zu tun.

Aber es war dann schön, dass ich ihnen diese Stellvertreterrolle am Ende noch aufgedrückt habe. Und dann hatte ich wieder meine Bananenrepublik.

Stefanie Popp ist Künstlerin und lebt in Köln.

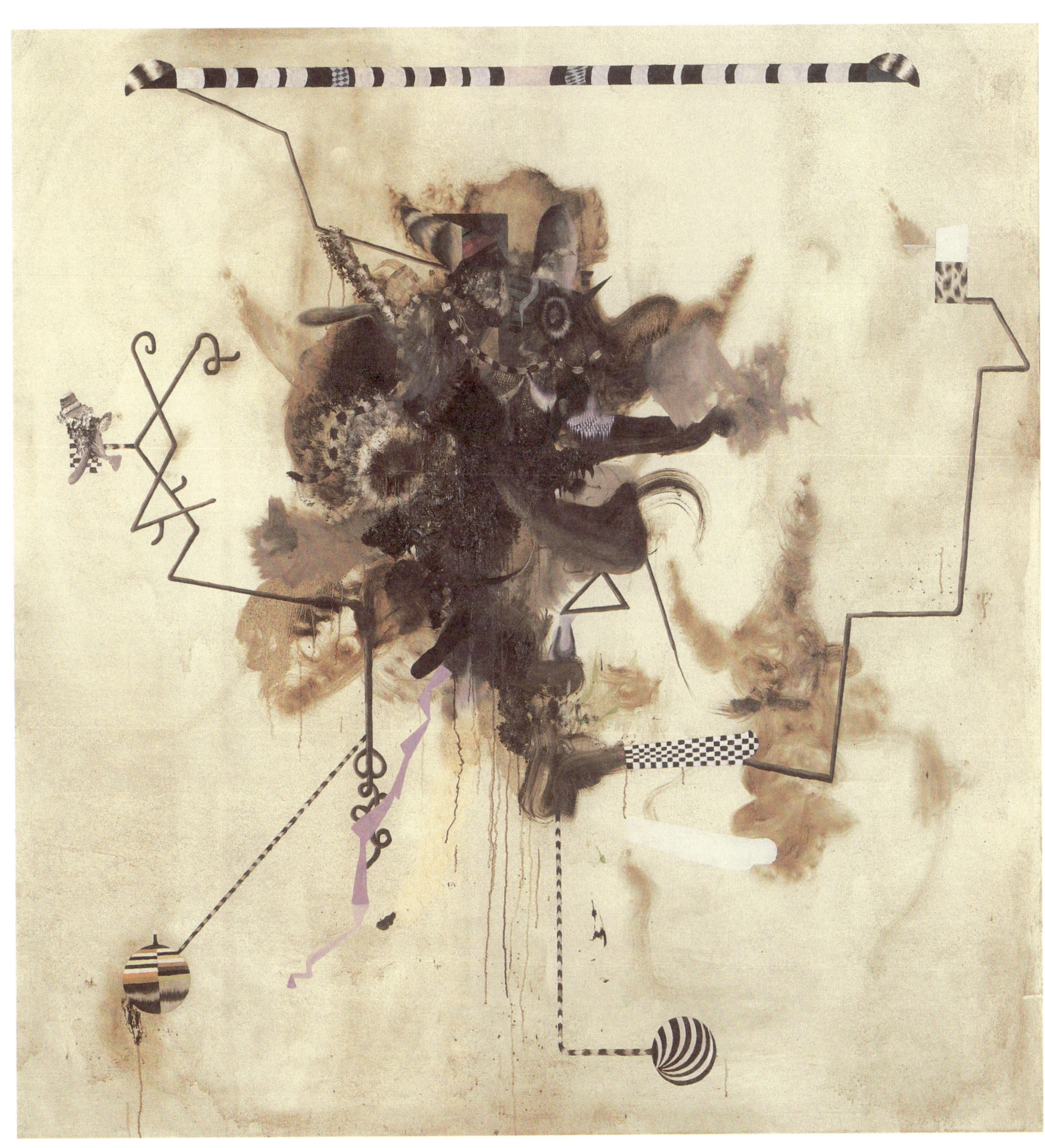

Jona Lewie–20 Million Years, 2007, oil on canvas, 200 x 190 cm

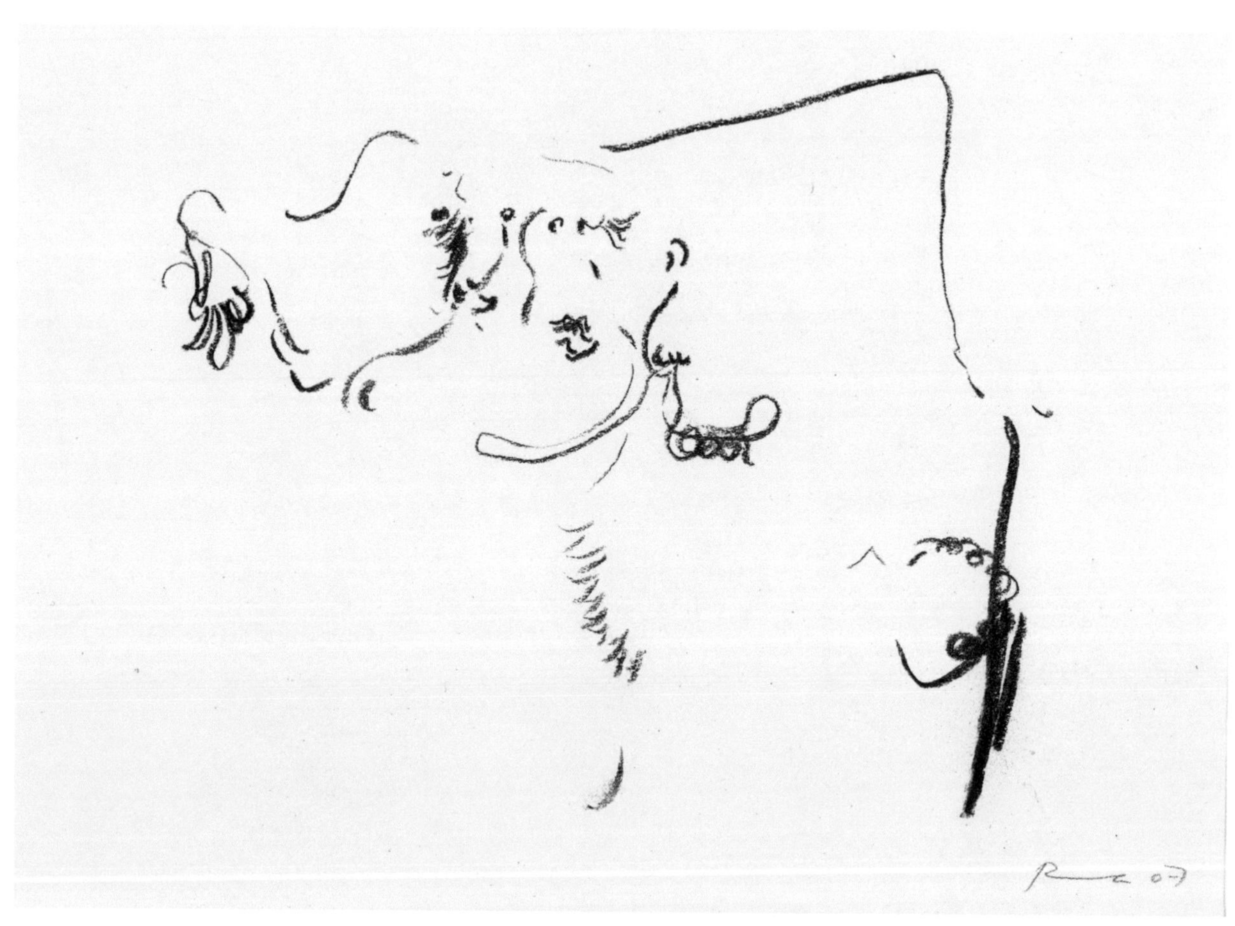

Untitled, 2007, charcoal on paper, 21 x 29.7 cm

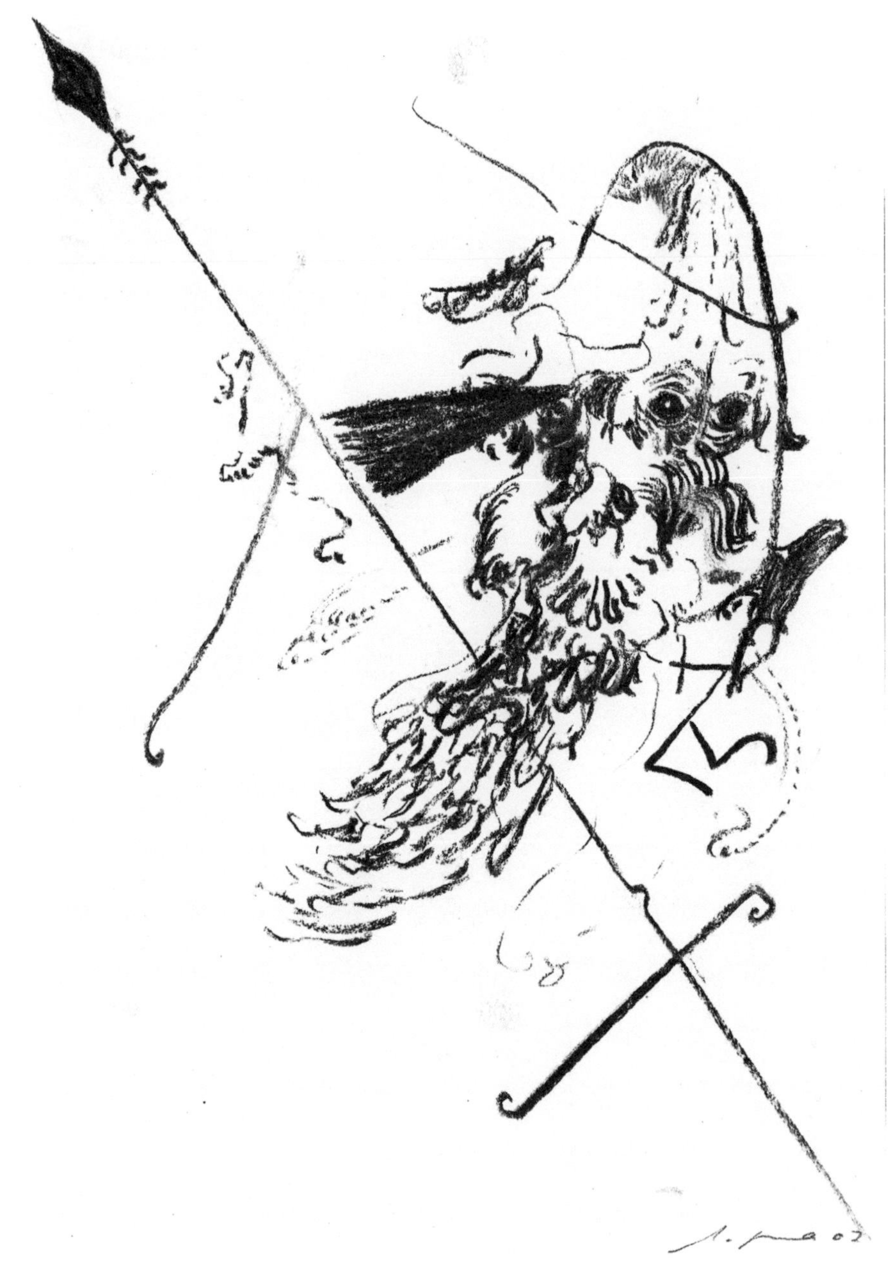

Untitled, 2007, charcoal on paper, 29.7 x 21 cm

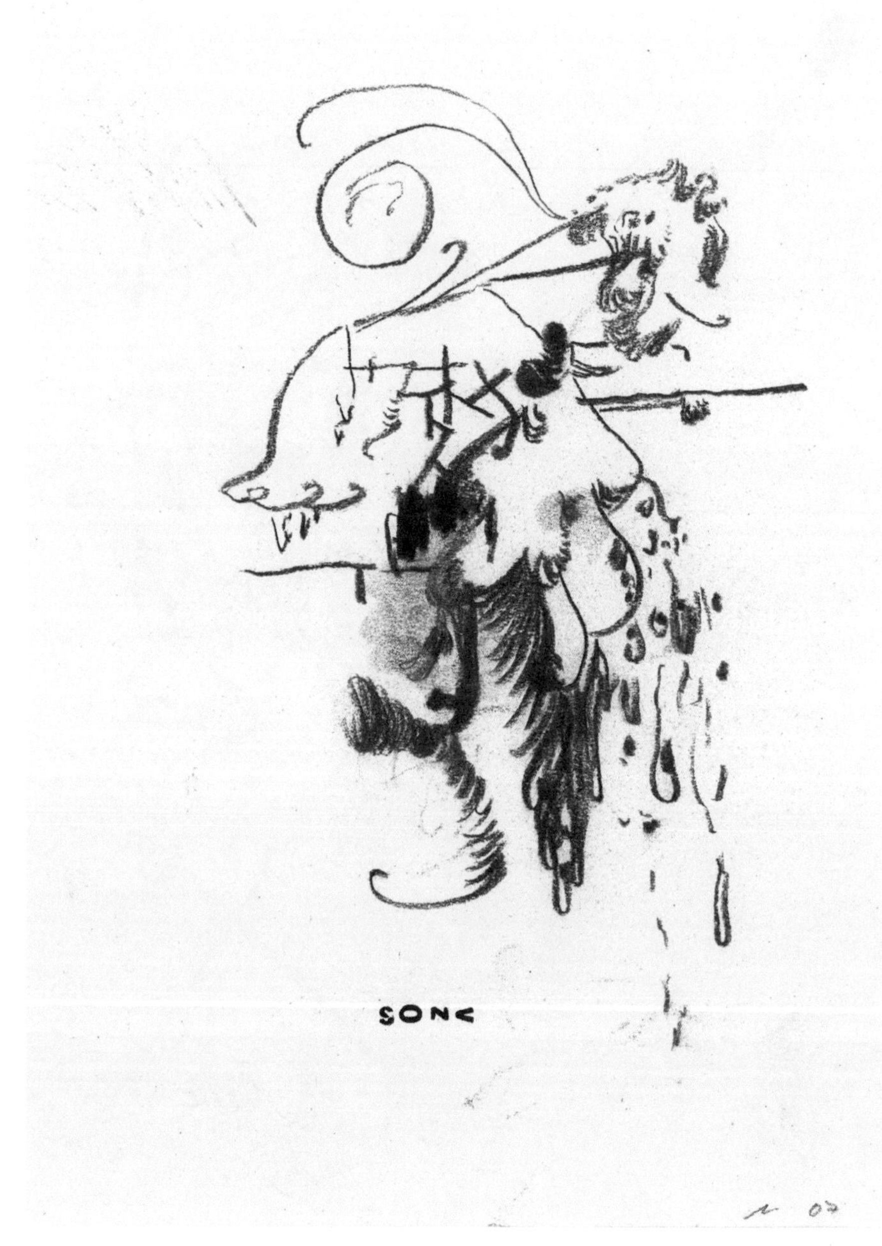

Mette, 2007, charcoal on paper, 29.7 x 21 cm

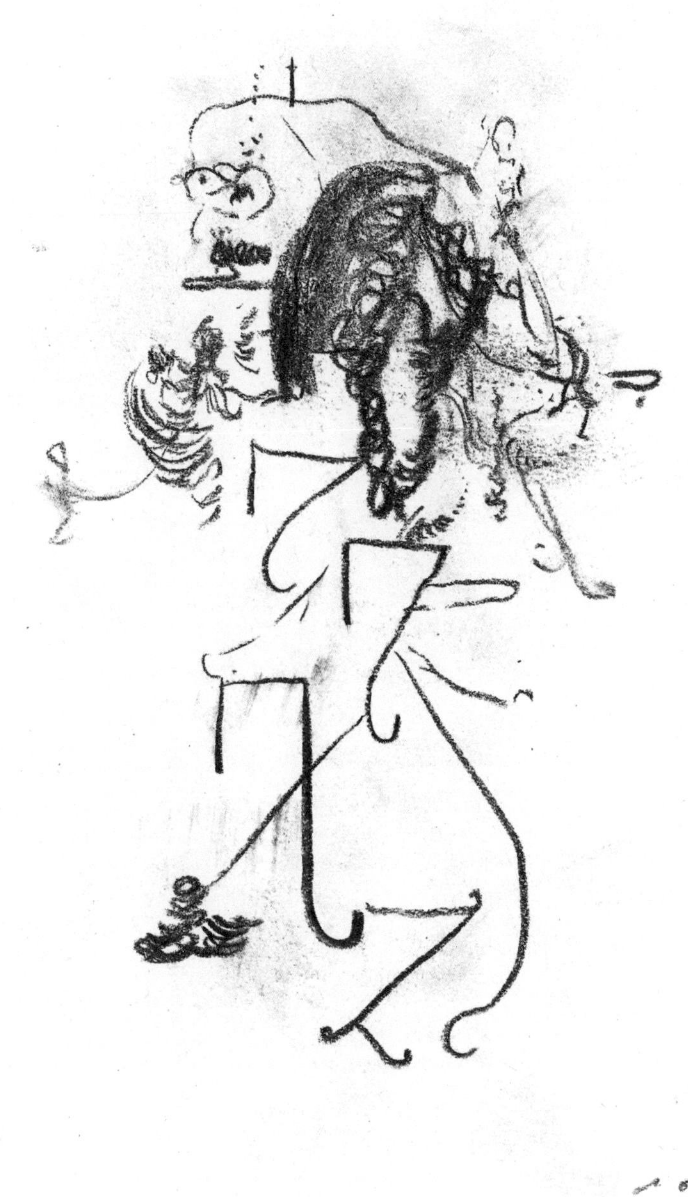

Nonnon, 2007, charcoal on paper, 29.7 x 21 cm

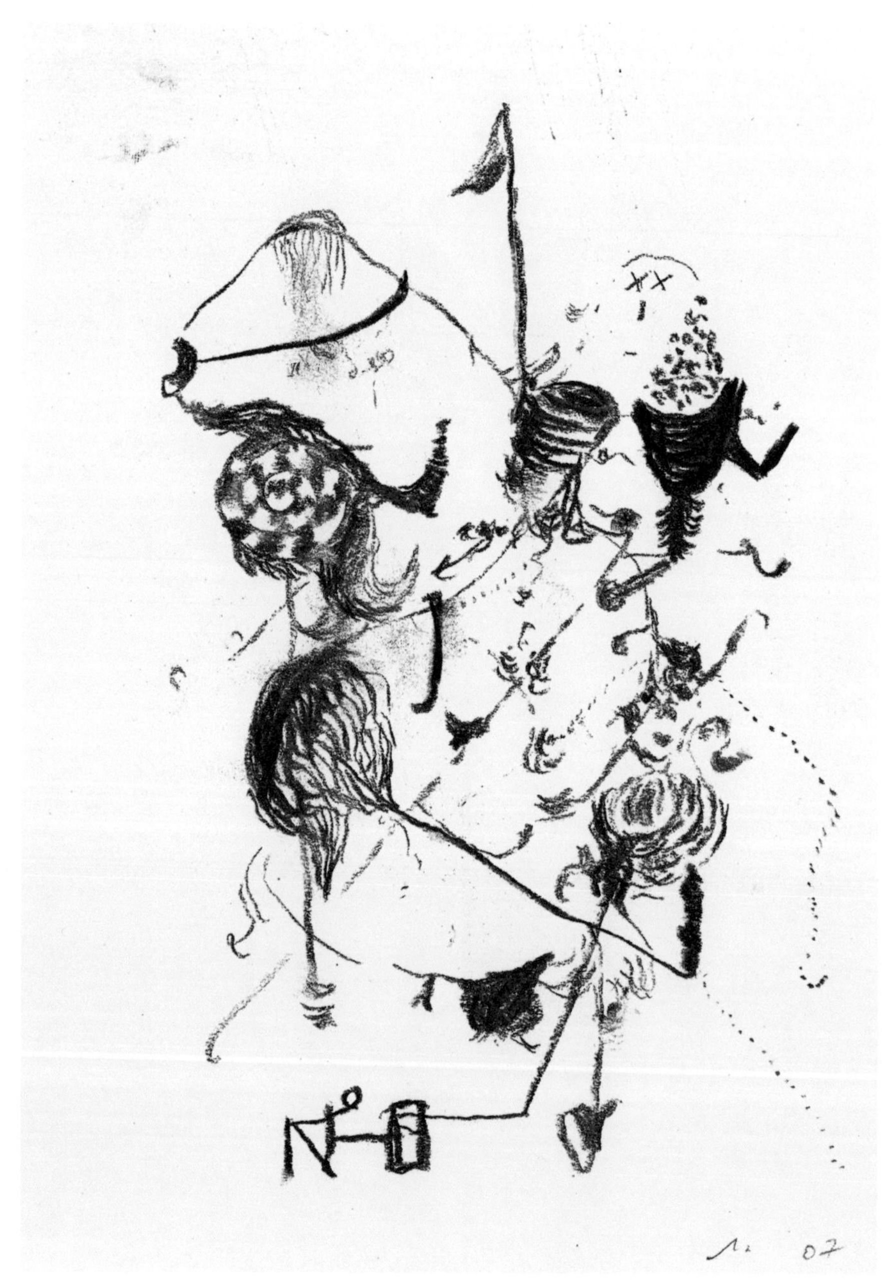

Lois Moon, 2007, charcoal on paper, 29.7 x 21 cm

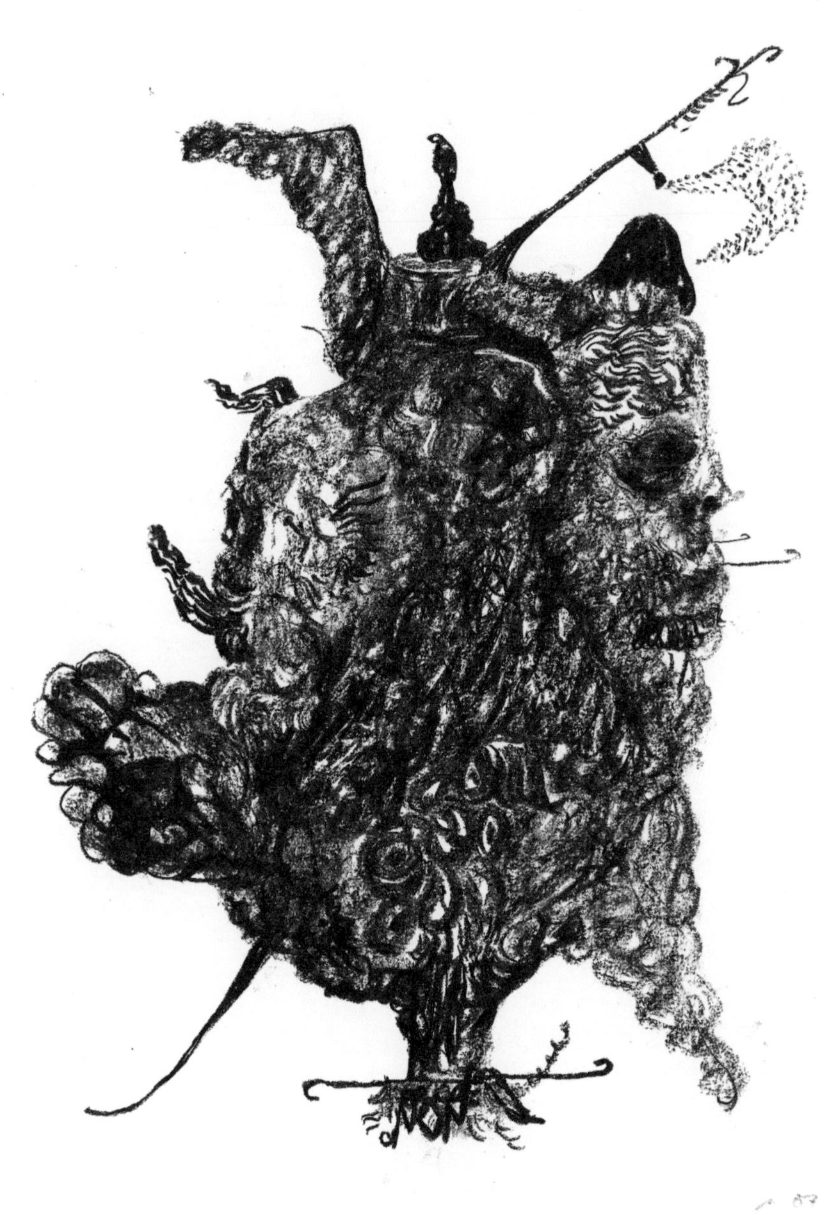

Für die Bäume, 2007, charcoal on paper, 42 x 29.7 cm

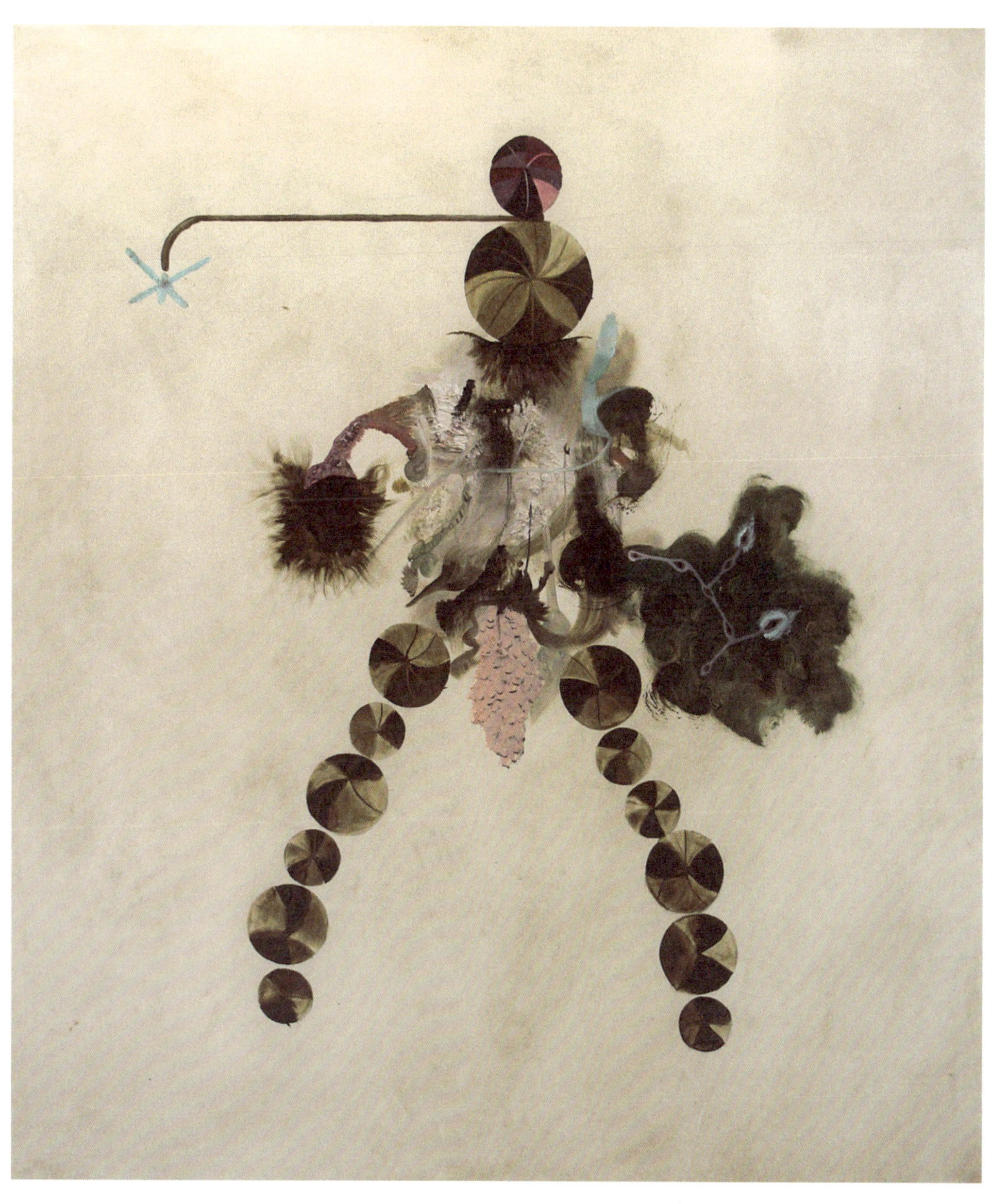

Tralla Pappa, 2006, oil on canvas, 150 x 130 cm

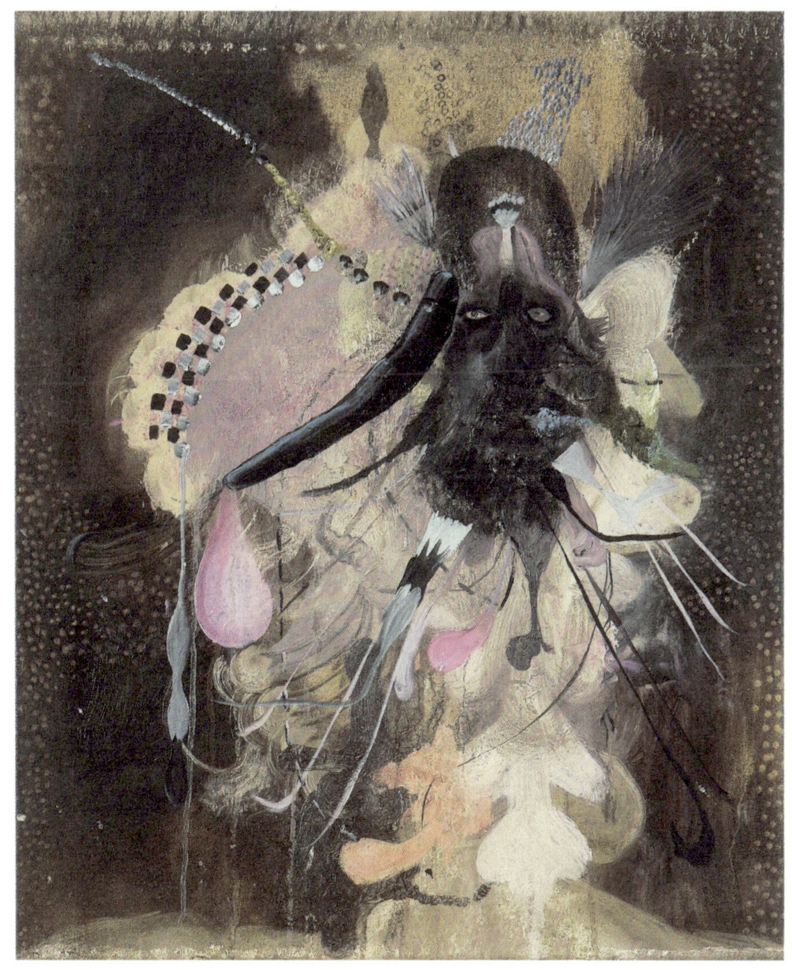

Jennifer Mob, 2006, oil on canvas, 60 x 50 cm

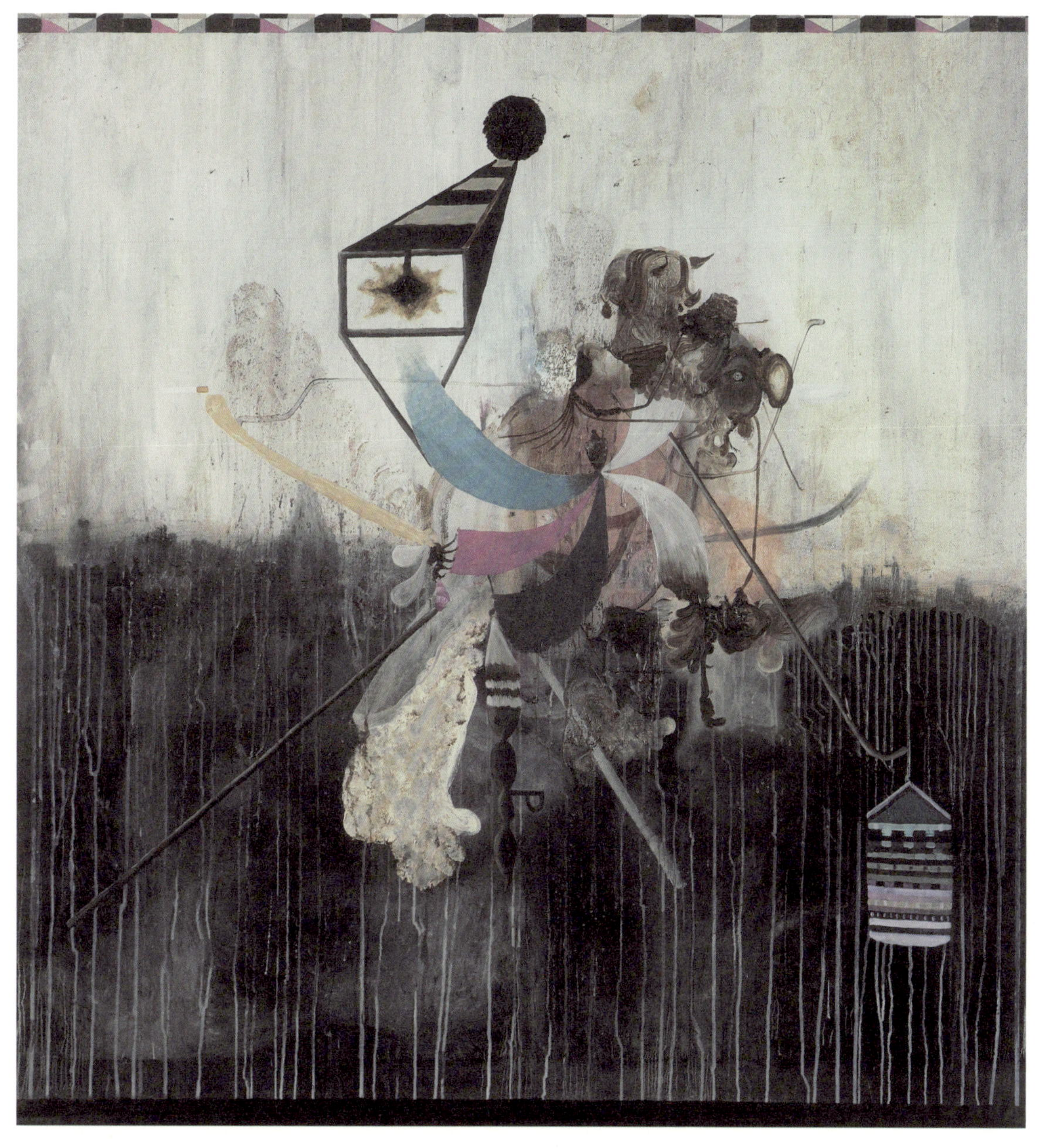

Ludger, 2006, oil on canvas, 160 x 150 cm

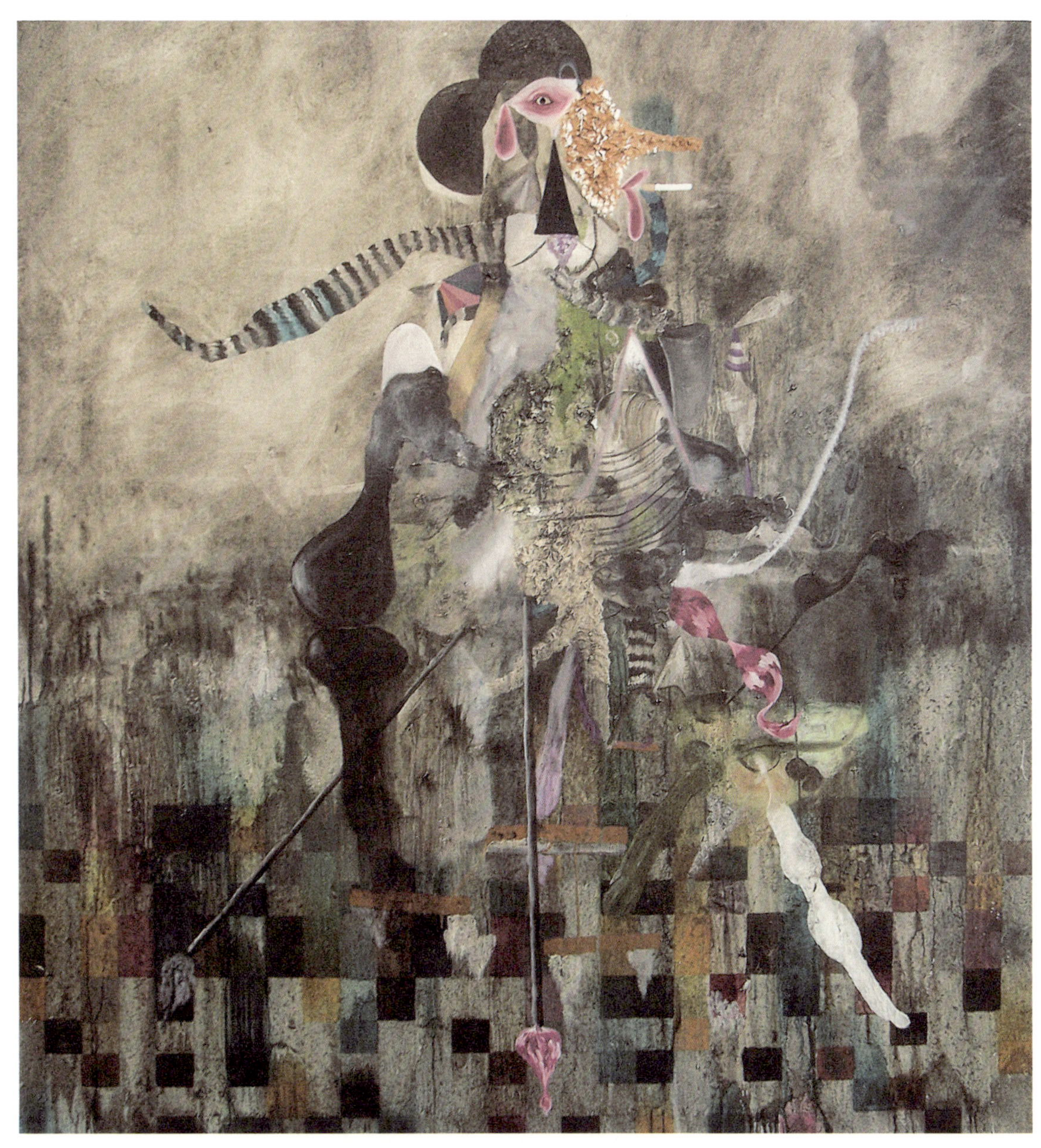

Uhli, 2006, oil on canvas, 160 x 150 cm

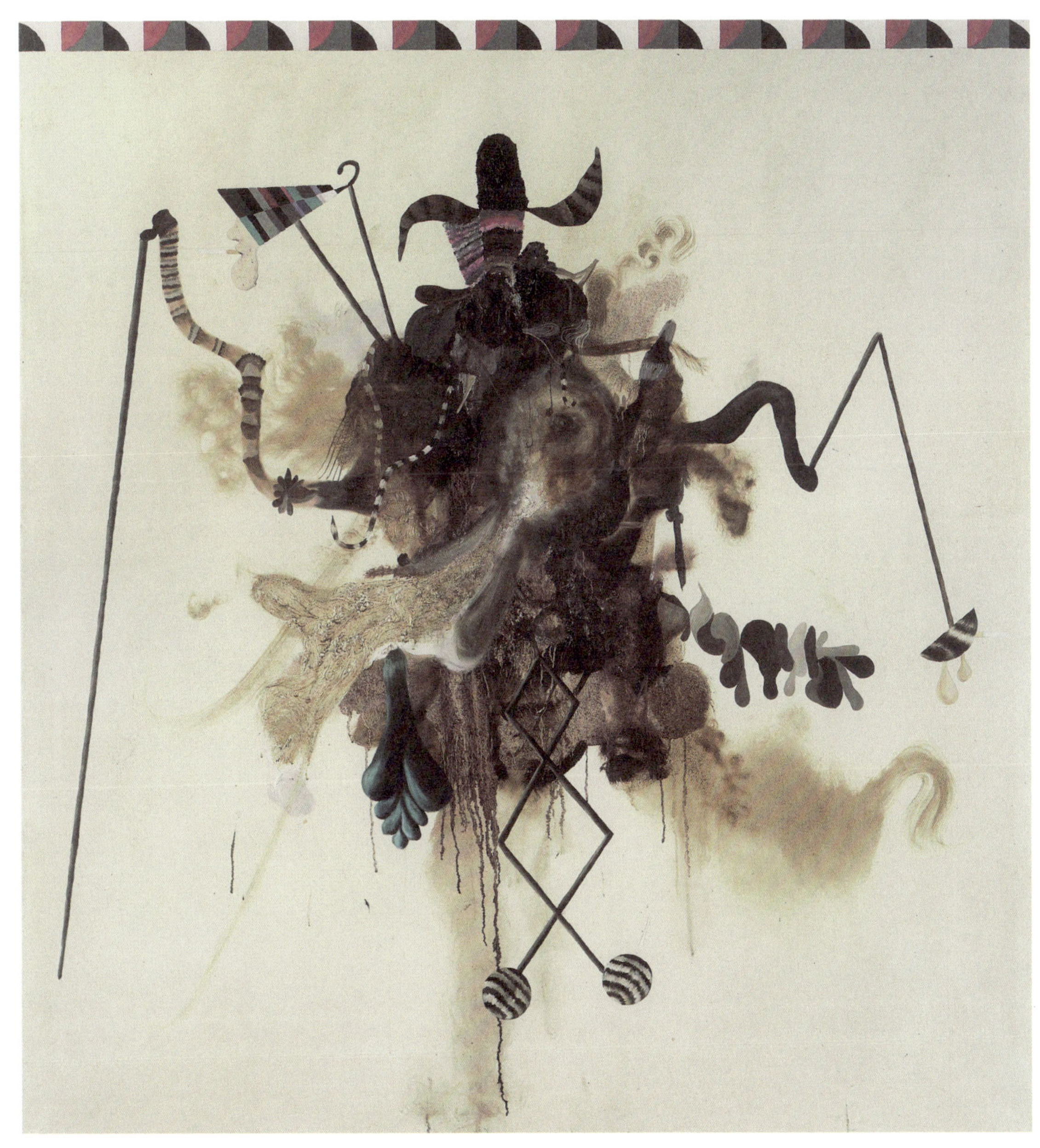

Roohm, 2007, oil on canvas, 160 x 150 cm

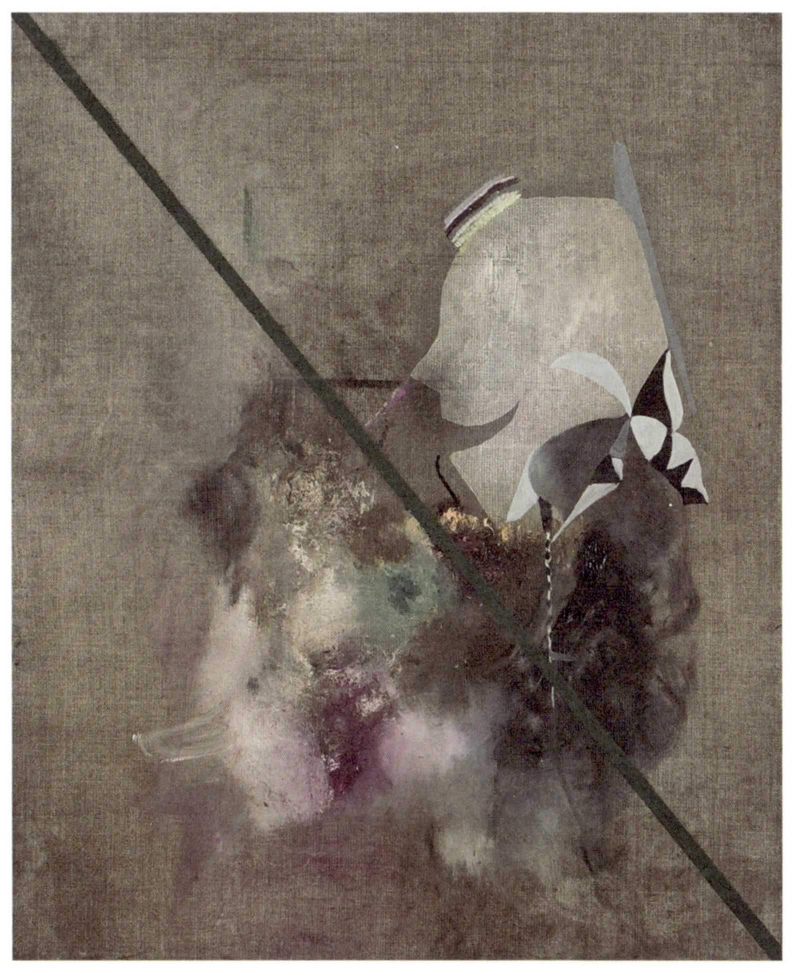

Freund 2–englisch, 2008, oil on canvas, 60 x 50 cm

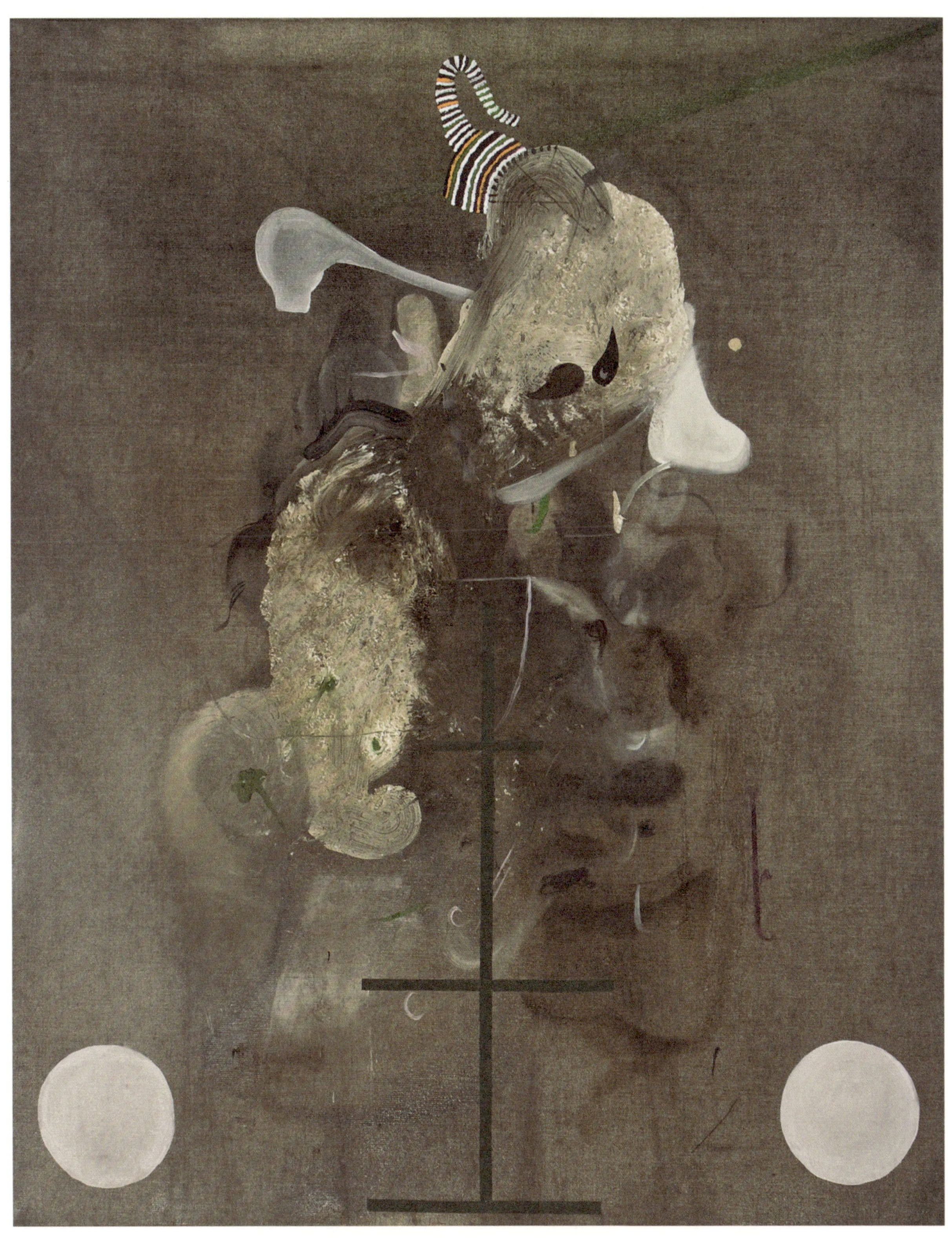

Untitled, 2008, oil on canvas, 100 x 80 cm

Michael Bauer
1973 born in Erkelenz, Germany
Lives and works in Cologne, Germany

p. 3 *Bad Harvest,* 2008 – Collection The Saatchi Gallery, London
p. 5 *Bosskopp,* 2008 – Private collection, New York
p. 6 *Pol 3, (Kamerad Säckle)* 2005 – Collection Jane and Richard Found, London
p. 7 *Pol 1, (Smart Estrus)* 2005 – Collection The Saatchi Gallery, London
p. 9 *Mungo Jerry,* 2006 – Private collection, London
p. 10 *Freund 1 – deutsch,* 2008 – Collection The Saatchi Gallery, London
p. 11 *L.O.R.D.S. 8000 (der alte Haw Haw)* 2006 – Private collection, Amsterdam
p. 12 *DJ El Tomorrow,* 2008 – courtesy the artist/Hotel, London
p. 13 *JMJ MOB,* 2008 – courtesy the artist/Hotel, London
p. 14 *No Opa,* 2008 – courtesy the artist/Hotel, London
p. 15 *Team Kimbo,* 2008 – courtesy the artist/Hotel, London
p. 16 *Ogerrock,* 2008 – courtesy the artist/Hotel, London
p. 17 *Borwasser,* 2008 – courtesy the artist/Hotel, London
p. 18 *Nonboy,* 2008 – courtesy the artist/Hotel, London
p. 19 *Oi Gabba,* 2008 – courtesy the artist/Hotel, London
p. 20 *Gobbit,* 2008 – courtesy the artist/Hotel, London
p. 21 *FMBM,* 2008 – courtesy the artist/Hotel, London
p. 25 *L.O.R.D.S. 7000 (der neue Haw-Haw),* 2006 – Collection GFL, Paris
p. 26 *Untitled,* 2007 – courtesy the artist/Galerie Peter Kilchmann, Zurich
p. 27 *Empe Gibson,* 2007 – courtesy the artist/Galerie Peter Kilchmann, Zurich
p. 28 *Charriot,* 2007 – courtesy the artist/Hotel, London
p. 29 *Untitled,* 2007 – courtesy the artist/Galerie Peter Kilchmann, Zurich
p. 31 *LORDS 3000,* 2006 – Collection The Saatchi Gallery, London
p. 33 *LORDS 4000,* 2006 – Collection The Saatchi Gallery, London
p. 34 *Doof Gallery,* 2007 – courtesy the artist/Galerie Peter Kilchmann, Zurich
p. 35 *Untitled,* 2007 – courtesy the artist/Galerie Peter Kilchmann, Zurich
p. 37 *SUBSTITUTE 3,* 2007 – Private collection, Moscow
p. 39 *B/M–YLMAZ–UHOS,* 2007 – courtesy the artist/Galerie Peter Kilchmann, Zurich
p. 41 *F/M–B/M 80 Million Years,* 2007 – Collection Südhausbau, Munich
p. 43 *B/M–B–Magneta,* 2007 – Private collection, New York
p. 45 *F/M SVORBEN,* 2007 – Private collection, Cologne
p. 46 *Untitled,* 2008 – courtesy the artist/Hotel, London
p. 47 *Untitled,* 2008 – courtesy the artist/Hotel, London
p. 53 *Prizcillaz,* 2006 – Collection of Burt Aaron, Michigan
p. 54 *Shake Your Libido,* 2007 – courtesy the artist/Hotel, London
p. 55 *Wolfberg,* 2007 – courtesy the artist/Hotel, London
p. 56 *Einer von Norden,* 2007 – courtesy the artist/Hotel, London
p. 57 *Einer von Westen,* 2007 – courtesy the artist/Hotel, London
p. 59 *Indianapolis,* 2006 – Private collection, Austria
p. 60 *Sandi,* 2004 – Boros Collection, Berlin
p. 61 *Mandi,* 2004 – Boros Collection, Berlin
p. 63 *Graf Bernadotte Indien,* 2004 – Private collection, Belgium
p. 64 *DJ Muppins Infinity,* 2007 – Collection Zabludowicz, London
p. 66 *DJ Penize,* 2007 – courtesy the artist/Galerie Peter Kilchmann, Zurich
p. 68 *DJ Pennydenny B,* 2007 – Collection Peter Kilchmann, Zurich
p. 70 *DJ Ponyhotello,* 2007 – Private collection, Athens
p. 72 *Burzum,* 2008 – courtesy the artist/Galerie Peter Kilchmann, Zurich
p. 75 *Harry Booth,* 2006 – Private collection, London
p. 77 *Nobsi Mob,* 2006 – Collection Dimitri Goulandris, London
p. 79 *Blair Petri, - 20 Million years* 2007
p. 81 *Basho Mob,* 2007 – courtesy the artist/Galerie Peter Kilchmann, Zurich
p. 83 *Bessy,* 2006 – Collection GFL, Paris
p. 95 *Jona Lewie,–20 Million Years* 2007 – courtesy the artist/Galerie Peter Kilchmann, Zurich
p. 96 *Untitled,* 2007 – courtesy the artist/Galerie Peter Kilchmann, Zurich
p. 97 *Untitled,* 2007 – courtesy the artist/Galerie Peter Kilchmann, Zurich
p. 98 *Mette,* 2007 – courtesy the artist/Hotel, London
p. 99 *Nonnon,* 2007 – courtesy the artist/Hotel London
p. 100 *Lois Moon,* 2007 – courtesy the artist/Hotel, London
p. 101 *Für die Bäume,* 2007 – courtesy the artist/Hotel, London
p. 103 *Tralla Pappa,* 2006 – Collection Bernier-Eliades Gallery, Athens
p. 105 *Jennifer Mob,* 2006 – Collection Steven Claydon, London
p. 107 *Ludger,* 2006 – Private collection, USA
p. 109 *Uhli,* 2006 – Private collection, USA
p. 111 *Roohm,* 2007 – Private collection, USA
p. 113 *Freund 2–englisch,* 2008 Collection The Saatchi Gallery, London
p. 115 *Untitled,* 2008 – Collection Silvie Fleming, London

Editors: Michael Bauer and Marcus Werner Hed
Co-produced by Hotel and Galerie Peter Kilchmann
Editorial Coordination: Annemarie Reichen
Proofreading: Louise Stein and Birte Theiler
Translations: Nicolas Grindell and Clemens Krümmel
Writing: Jennifer Higgie
Interview: Stefanie Popp

Art Direction: Marcus Werner Hed
Design: Jennifer Campbell-Colquhoun
Photographer: p. 7, 9, 14, 16, 17, 26-27, 50, 51, 119, Thomas Müller
p. 29, 31, 38, 41, 43, 45, 47, 49, 68-77, A. Burger
p. 99, Livio Baumgartner, p. 30, 33, 39, 100 Barbora Gerny
Typeset in New Century Schoolbook
Cover image: Michael Bauer 2008
Production: Musumeci S.p.A., Quart (Aosta)

Published by
JRP | Ringier
Letzigraben 134
CH-8047 Zurich
T +41 (0) 43 311 27 50
F +41 (0) 43 311 27 51
www.jrp-ringier.com
info@jrp-ringier.com

ISBN 978-3-905829-85-3

JRP | Ringier publications are available internationally at selected
bookstores and from the following distribution partners:

Switzerland
Buch 2000, AVA Verlagsauslieferung AG, Centralweg 16,
CH-8910 Affoltern a.A., buch2000@ava.ch, www.ava.ch

Germany and Austria
Vice Versa Vertrieb, Immanuelkirchstrasse 12, D-10405 Berlin
info@vice-versa-vertrieb.de, www.vice-versa-vertrieb.de

France
Les Presses du réel, 35 rue Colson, F-21000 Dijon
info@lespressesdureel.com, www.lespressesdureel.com

UK and other European countries
Cornerhouse Publications, 70 Oxford Street, UK-Manchester M1 5NH
publications@cornerhouse.org, www.cornerhouse.org/books

USA, Canada, Asia, and Australia
D.A.P./Distributed Art Publishers, 155 Sixth Avenue, 2nd Floor
USA-New York, NY 10013, dap@dapinc.com, www.artbook.com

For a list of our partner bookshops or for any general questions
please contact JRP | Ringier directly at info@jrp-ringier.com, or visit our
homepage www.jrp-ringier.com for further information about our program.

Thanks to: Stefanie Popp, Jennifer Higgie, Marcus Werner Hed,
Lionel Bovier, Darren Flook, Christabel Stewart, Peter Kilchmann,
Annemarie Reichen, Margherita Hohenlohe, Jennifer Campbell-Colquhoun,
Philipp Fernandes do Brito, Robert Kraiss, Florian Gass,
Michaela Eichwald, Lisa Cooley, Johnny Whitmer, David Noonan,
Steven Claydon, Thomas Viney, Boris Brandts, Marte Eknaes,
Susanne Zander, Nicole Delmes, Ellen Gronwald, Hartmut Neumann,
Walter Dahn, Georg Bauer, Karin Bauer, Claudia Bauer, Daniela A'Brassard.